The Journey to Happy

How Embracing the Concept That <u>Nothing Is Wrong</u>
Can Transform Your Life
Or
How I Went from Being Unhappy, Overweight,
and in a Job I Hated to Being Happy, Achieving My
Ideal Weight, and Doing Work That I Love...
and How YOU Can, Too!

- **Find Out** - **Clear Out** - **Bliss Out**

Walk the 9 Stepping Stones on the Journey to Happy
Are you ready to walk the path?

Happiness

The Journey to Happy

How Embracing the Concept That <u>Nothing Is Wrong</u>
Can Transform Your Life

First Edition: October 19th, 2016. (Updated: 7-29-2017)
Proudly printed in the USA.
Published by: Abundant Press - www.AbundantPress.com

Trademarks
All terms mentioned in this book that are known to be trademarks or service marks have been appropriately capitalized. Trademarks belong to the appropriate companies.

ISBN: 978-0-9977561-2-8

Abundant Press
Publish - Promote - Profit - Position - Present

This book is Interactive!
Download Your 6 Free Bonus Videos Now!

This book is interactive! I am thrilled to show you how to bring it to life. All the QR (Quick Response) codes throughout the book (see the one below) can be scanned with your Smartphone or iPad to watch the videos that were created especially for you.

How to Scan the QR Codes in This Book

Step 1:
Download a *free* QR code reader onto your smartphone by searching the App Store. I selected the Kaywa Reader because it is free of advertisements.

Step 2:
Tap the app once it has downloaded to your phone; this will open up the Reader. Tap again, and your camera will appear to be on. Hover over the code you wish to scan, and the camera will automatically take a picture of the QR code; then your phone will be directed to the respective web page on **http:// SedonaSoulAdventures.com** that contains each message. I've also included each url.

Let's start with the **6 Free Bonus Videos** that my online readers downloaded. You can download them here:

1. **Embracing the Concept of Nothing Is Wrong**

   or go to: http://thejourneytohappy.com/video1/

2. **Get Happy Right Now**

   or go to: http://thejourneytohappy.com/video2/

3. **Find Out, Clear Out, Bliss Out** (a proven process to happy!)

   or go to: http://thejourneytohappy.com/video3/

4. **Sedona Chakra Meditation** (clear & balance your chakras)

   or go to: http://thejourneytohappy.com/video4/

5. **The 51% Rule** (it's easier to get happy than you might think)

or go to: http://thejourneytohappy.com/video5/

6. **The Sedona Effect** (find out how this can transform your life!)

or go to: http://thejourneytohappy.com/video6/

And watch for more interesting videos throughout the book. Enjoy!

Table of Contents

Dedication

For Everyone at
Sedona Soul Adventures

You continue to amaze me
every single day

Welcome to the Journey to Happy
How Embracing the Concept That <u>Nothing Is Wrong</u> Can Transform Your Life

Welcome to a new way of looking at your life!

Does even the concept that *Nothing Is Wrong* make your head spin?

Do you feel like you're about to fall down a rabbit hole?

It can feel that way when you are about to embark on a different way of approaching things, a different way of speaking about things, and a different way of doing things. It can be a little disorienting.

But that's a wonderful place to start! Let yourself feel a little off balance.

It makes it easier to get yourself out of the places where you're stuck.

The true purpose of this book is to take you out of your mindset that makes you tell yourself that you're stuck in an unhappy life, an unhappy relationship, and unfulfilling work, and you're dissatisfied with your physical body and money situation. Shifting out of that mindset is the first step towards getting yourself unstuck and from there it's absolutely amazing what can happen!

It took me so many years to discover and finally implement the awareness and processes that I'm going to be sharing with you. What's stupefying is that even after I first learned the ideas here, it took me another ten years to figure out how to implement them. After I finally learned how to implement the principles you will learn here, the results were astounding!

I went from:

- being depressed to being happy
- being 40 pounds overweight to achieving my ideal weight
- being $50,000 in debt to financial abundance
- hating the work I was doing to doing work that I LOVE

The most wonderful part about all of this is that it's so simple. The ideas and truths in this book have been around for years, and everything I'm suggesting is very easy to do. Even better, you already know how to do everything in this book. You're just not doing it. Transforming your mindset to the attitude of *Nothing Is Wrong* is what the Journey to Happy is all about.

INTRODUCTION

How Can You Get The Most Out Of This Book?

I've been working with people during difficult parts of their lives for over 30 years. For 20 of those years, I was a family law attorney in Omaha, Nebraska where I represented thousands of people going through a divorce, which is one of the most difficult experiences that can ever happen in a person's life. In 1999, I visited Sedona, Arizona for the first time and had a spiritual reawakening and realization that it was time to change my life, and I will be talking about that experience in later chapters. That led me on a three-year journey of personal healing with the amazing practitioners in Sedona until I finally moved there in 2001. Six months later, I founded Sedona Soul Adventures where we do private, customized retreats for individuals and couples.

Together with over 40 of the most incredible and experienced healers Sedona has to offer, I've been involved in this work now for over 14 years – and what happens is almost unbelievable! People come to us burned out, stressed out, unhappy, depressed, in deep emotional pain, and sometimes feeling like they're at the end of their rope. Many couples come to us on the verge of divorce.

After going through our Sedona Proven Process, individuals leave happy, content, and at peace knowing their life's purpose and ready to live it. Couples are able to let go of the resentments of the past, rediscover the love that brought them together in the first place, and bring the sizzle back into their relationship.

It's ironic to me that I was a divorce attorney for 20 years, and now I've done so much to save and renew countless marriages. Even after 14 years and helping thousands of people, I'm still amazed at what happens.

It was working through my own personal healing process and doing sessions with many of the amazing practitioners in Sedona that brought me to the teachings that are in this book. I try to live this all day, every day. Do I do it perfectly? No, I don't. I'm human.

Will *you* live it all day, every day? Probably not. You're also human. Part of what I teach throughout this book is the invaluable lesson of compassion for yourself. Human imperfection notwithstanding, as you put these principles into practice, you'll discover results that are almost miraculous.

You see, through all of my years of working with people, I've found that everyone is pretty much looking for the same things: happiness, contentment, and peace. Most people think it will be the result of having some "thing" or combination of "things" – the great job, the fantastic relationship, the perfect body, lots of money – so they're constantly on a quest to find or change the "thing" that they believe will finally make them happy.

What they don't seem to understand is that they're really looking for happiness itself – and that's not to be found in "things".

Now, don't get me wrong. This book is NOT advocating that you shouldn't want things. This book is about how to allow these things to flow to you even more quickly and easily by coming into the energy of Nothing Is Wrong so that you can finally experience the peace and happiness for which you've been searching.

How Can You Get the Most Out of This Book?

In each chapter, we'll explore a different area of your life, and I'll show you the important truth that Nothing Is Wrong. Nothing is Wrong with you, other people (even the ones who drive you crazy), your life, your body, your money situation, your work, your relationships, or even with the world in general. Embracing that truly is the journey to the happiness that you seek.

We'll be discussing concepts that go as far back as the Bible and ideas that are emerging as part of the new Quantum Physics (the easy stuff, not the complicated stuff).

As you read, you will become aware that the book is put together in such a way that allows you to:

1. **Find Out** about the things that may be holding you back,
2. **Clear Out** the thoughts and energy and emotional gunk that are keeping you stuck, and
3. **Bliss Out** and live your life from a place of happiness and contentment by knowing (and deeply believing) that Nothing Is Wrong.

I've chosen this format because it's the basis of the Sedona Proven Process that has helped thousands of individuals and couples who have experienced a Sedona Soul Adventures retreat. With the process of Find Out, Clear Out, and Bliss Out, people have transformed their lives and relationships and have taken home the tools they need to apply it in their daily lives. I want to help you to have a taste of that, too.

While reading about transformation is not the same as experiencing a retreat of 3-5 days of one-on-one sessions with our phenomenal practitioners in the amazing transformational energy of Sedona, this information plus my **Nine Stepping**

Stones on the Journey to Happy that I give you can help you start moving into the energy of peace and happiness and contentment – *starting right now!*

If you haven't already, watch my video *"Find Out, Clear Out, Bliss Out"*

or go to: http://thejourneytohappy.com/video3/

Use my Nine Stepping Stones on the Journey to Happy

I'm also thrilled to introduce to you the proven and absolutely powerful concept of my **Nine Stepping Stones on the Journey to Happy** – nine processes designed to bring you into the happiness and connection you're craving.

In each chapter, I'll share processes to help you implement and integrate the ideas we're discussing. At first, they may seem rather simple, but as you begin to understand precisely how to use them, you'll discover that they're astonishingly powerful.

As I said earlier, **these are things that you already know how to do**; it's simply a matter of taking just a little bit of time to think and ponder and feel. The Stepping Stones have a cumulative effect – one leads to the next and takes you along the path to happiness and contentment.

Here's a preview of my **Nine Stepping Stones on the Journey to Happy**. Of course, I discuss them in much more detail in subsequent chapters, but to give you a feel for what's coming, here they are in brief:

1. **What's Your Story? Find Out What's Wrong**. Making a list of everything that you are telling yourself is wrong brings everything into your conscious awareness and is profoundly cathartic.

2. **Change Your Story, Change Your Life**. It can be shocking to discover what happens when you stop talking about all of your problems all of the time and start focusing on the good aspects of your life.

3. **The Enneagram.** You might not be familiar with the Enneagram at this point, but I will tell you that it is one of the most potent and powerful of the many processes I have used over the past 30+ years. The Enneagram is a personality analysis and inventory that has been in existence for over 1,000 years. In fact, the Crusaders brought it back to Europe after discovering it in the Middle East.

The results of this simple test will tell you how you are wired to automatically have certain ideas and similar reactions in different areas of your life. When people are first exposed to the Enneagram, they typically have a response that is jaw dropping. It explains so much about you and your relationship to other people! As you go through the chapter devoted to the Enneagram, you'll take the test and discover some things about yourself that will have a huge impact on how you interact with yourself and with others.

If you are already familiar with the Enneagram, I think you'll love how I've woven it into all aspects of your life – your relationship with yourself and how this affects your body, your money situation, your work, your relationships with other people, and even how you view the world – in each chapter of the book. Even after all of these years of using this extraordinary tool, I'm still amazed at the insights it produces.

4. **What Are the Patterns That You (Unconsciously) Took on from Your Parents (Teachers, Caregivers) That Are Continuing to Impact You Today?** When I first did this process many years ago, I was so shocked! Until we look at the different areas that I discuss in this chapter, we don't even realize we're doing this. And it's not about blaming your parents. Remember that Nothing Is Wrong with your parents! It's just that bringing this information into your conscious awareness can be life changing. It was for me.

5. **"Loving Your Body" Meditation.** After battling my weight my entire life, I lost 40 pounds with this one simple process – without dieting or exercise – and effortlessly went from a size 14 to a size 6. I now continue to eat and drink whatever I want whenever I want. I'll show you how to do the same.

6. **The Gratitude Journal.** One of the most powerful ways to bring abundance and contentment into your life is to actively practice gratitude. You may just want to jump ahead and start your Gratitude Journal now because it works with everything – money, body, relationships – everything.

7. **Tapping.** If you haven't experienced the transformational power of tapping, prepare to be amazed. Entire books exist that are dedicated entirely to tapping, but I've condensed everything you need to know about this simple but powerful process into a single chapter so that you can start using it and benefitting from it right now! As with the other Stepping Stones, Tapping is a phenomenal process for any issue that you are grappling with and has even been shown to help with anxiety, phobias, and depression.

8. **Affirmations.** If you think Affirmations are too basic and simple, then think again! Most people aren't practicing Affirmations the correct way, and, in some situations when done incorrectly, they are doing more harm than good. Learn the exact way to rewire your brain using Affirmations.

9. **Deep Breathing Meditation.** Our breath is our fastest and closest connection to the Divine and to the energy of All That Is. Use this powerful five-minute technique to achieve instant calm. It is the quickest and most effective way on the planet to **Bliss Out**.

Get a Journal or Notebook

If you really commit to doing the work described in this book, follow the recommendations throughout the book to write or journal. I recommend that you get a journal or notebook right away. Don't recycle an old one that you have lying around; it has old energy on it, the energy of things being wrong. Get a new one! It can be as simple as an inexpensive notebook that you find at Walgreens or CVS or, if you like, buy a beautiful journal that makes you feel good when you look at it. After all, this is all about you feeling good.

Read a New Chapter Every Three Days

If you read a new chapter every three days, you will complete the book and the processes in 30 days.

Keep Incorporating Each Stepping Stone as You Move Along the Path

The chapters of this book are set up to do this so that you will more deeply integrate each Stepping Stone as you move along the path.

Remember That Each Stepping Stone Can Be Used for Each Issue

The beauty of the Stepping Stones is that each of them is applicable and usable for any issue. For example, although the Gratitude Journal is introduced with the chapter on Money, the Gratitude Journal is fantastic for using with issues related to your body, your work, your relationships, etc.

Think About Getting The Journey to Happy Video Companion Course

I developed this 9 Video course to help you get the results you're looking for even faster, with less effort. If you'd like to check it out here:

or go to: http://thejourneytohappy.com/invite/

Allow Yourself to Feel Skeptical (or Whatever It Is You're Feeling)

As you read this book, you might find yourself experiencing a range of emotions, from skeptical to excited. *Nothing Is Wrong with that.* In my experience, skepticism can be vital to the process, and I encourage you to be skeptical about everything I say. Don't *believe* these teachings. Experience them. Feel them. Do they resonate with you? Do they feel true for you? A huge part of this book is about coming into connection with the Real You. What do you *really* think? What do you *really* believe? What feels right to YOU?

What If There Is Something in My Life That IS Definitely Wrong?

What if you have a serious illness? What if your spouse is cheating on you? What if you've lost a child? How can anyone say that Nothing Is Wrong in those circumstances?

Please know that I'm not making light of your difficulties. You'll discover during our time together that I have experienced many challenges in my own life, my dad's alcoholism, my mother's death at the age of 51, I was in a bad marriage, deep in debt, I have deep compassion for where you are, BUT I also know that there is a way out! **It was when I was at the lowest points in my life that things were able to shift for me.** And I'll tell you all about how that happened.

I'm NOT saying that everything is perfect. I'm not saying that you shouldn't feel grief, fear, anger, or outrage if any of those things are happening to you. What I AM saying is that by embracing some of these concepts, you can bring a level of peace to your life that wasn't there before. And, especially in the most difficult times in our lives, even a tiny bit of peace can change everything.

That's my prayer for you – even if you're in the depths of despair – to bring a tiny bit of peace. If you're living a life of "quiet desperation" (as Thoreau said), I want to show you how you can change things around and start along the path of living the life of your dreams.

Are you ready to walk the path? Then let's begin!

Debra Stangl
Sedona, Arizona

Happiness

CHAPTER I

EMBRACING THE CONCEPT THAT NOTHING IS WRONG

Have You Ever Asked Yourself, *"Why Are There Times When I Am So Unhappy?"*

There can be an almost infinite combination of life circumstances that causes unhappiness, but in the end, the answer is simple. When you are unhappy, it is because you think something is wrong.

Many people spend most of their lives in this place – unhappy with their circumstances, work, money, bodies, or husband/wife/children/family/friends.

It's easy to see how it happens. We're bombarded every day with media messages telling us that we should be better, thinner, richer, and happier when, in reality, this simply makes us even more unhappy and dissatisfied because we're comparing our lives to an impossible standard.

Here's a simple truth: at the root of everything you say you want (money, a nice home, satisfying work, a good marriage, perfect children) is a desire for peace and happiness. A feeling of contentment. That is what you are truly yearning for.

What if I told you that there's a secret to turning this around – a way for you to have lasting joy and happiness WITHOUT sacrificing the things you want and without going off to live in a cave in India? (And, of course, Nothing Is Wrong with living in a cave in India.)

It starts by letting go of the story that something is wrong and embracing the idea that everything is exactly as it should be.

How I Started Thinking That Something Was Wrong

I grew up thinking that something was wrong with me – well, not exactly wrong, but *off*. From the time I was 12 years old, my parents always seemed to be struggling. There were six children in our family, and even though we lived in a nice house and belonged to the country club and went to private school, money seemed to be a continual problem. I remember my mother's favorite saying: "Do you think I just go into the back yard and pick money off of a tree?" No, I didn't think that, but the thought was pretty wonderful.

My parents pushed my siblings and me to be more and do more so that we could (ultimately) have more. One of the heartbreaks of my mother's life was that she was not able to go to college. Her father had literally lost the farm during the Great Depression of the 1930s. While I was growing up, her constant mantra was that we were all going to go to college – the four boys so that they could be doctors and lawyers and my sister and me so that we could "catch" a doctor or lawyer and then be able to talk to the college-educated husbands we had ensnared.

We were continually "doing" things. The boys were involved with sports and their studies and Boy Scouts. Because my mother had always been fascinated by show business, I started taking dance at the age of three. The boys were expected to be

Eagle Scouts, and I was expected to be Miss America and then land a Hollywood contract. Alas, it didn't quite work out that way. My brothers never became Eagle Scouts, and I was never crowned Miss America, nor did I receive a Hollywood contract.

But, the lesson took hold and the good news is that we all did very well as adults. My four brothers became a doctor, a dentist, an engineer, and an extremely successful financial planner. I became an attorney. My sister (the creative one of whom we are all jealous) is a director of plays and operas and does fantastic productions all over the country. We all became Type A overachievers and, to this day, we all do too much because it was instilled in us that doing, doing, doing would get us what we wanted, and if we weren't doing, doing, doing, something was wrong.

And, according to my mother, something was always wrong. We all got good grades, but only one of us (Bob, the doctor) got straight A's. I never practiced my dancing enough. The boys never earned enough merit badges or excelled enough at sports.

When I was 13, my father's alcoholism started really showing up, and it took a toll on our entire family. His drinking led to deep money problems, and we almost lost everything. But, rather than change our lifestyle in light of our new circumstances, we kept "acting as if" everything was the same. We still lived in the nice house, still belonged to the country club, still went to private school, still took dance and golf and tennis lessons. My sister even got a horse. In fact, we didn't even call what was happening "alcoholism". We were told, "Dad has emotional problems that he deals with by drinking, but he goes to work, and he's not lying in the gutter, so he's not an alcoholic." In Alcoholics Anonymous that is called "denial" and "enabling".

So now, added to the general idea that something was wrong that could be fixed by studying hard and excelling at all the stuff we were doing, there was something that was actually wrong that we were covering up and not telling anyone about – something we were ashamed of.

I'm NOT saying that my mother didn't love us. She loved us and wanted the world for us! Her dreams and desires led us to be who we are today. But people can also excel from a condition of loving themselves and being happy. It's a lot more comfortable than continually dwelling on dissatisfaction.

I was a scared little girl who grew up into a scared big girl, who acted like she knew what she was doing, who looked successful, who put on a facade of control – when nothing was further from the truth. I was unhappy, dissatisfied, and constantly unable to shake the feeling that things would be different and better if only *I* could be different and better. *Then*, I thought, *I'd finally achieve happiness and peace!*

But that never happened until I finally discovered that it's not about being more or having more or doing more – it's in loving and appreciating what is happening NOW. It's in being grateful for your life. It's in understanding that Nothing Is Wrong, and not only is nothing wrong, but everything is exactly the way it should be.

Does that sound too strange to be true? Let me explain.

The Concept of Nothing Is Wrong – It's Not the Circumstances; It's Your Reaction to the Circumstances

At this point, I know that some of you are thinking, "Of course something is wrong! I don't have enough money, my marriage is on the rocks, and my kids are driving me crazy!" Well, just hang in there with me for a little bit. This paradigm shift just might revolutionize your life.

You see, our unhappiness doesn't come from outside circumstances. Our unhappiness comes from our *response and reaction* to outside circumstances.

You might be saying, "But everyone is unhappy when they don't have enough money/love/___ (fill in the blank with whatever it is you think you lack)." But is that really true? Don't you know people who don't have a lot of money who are happy? Have you seen the movie *"Happy"*? It's a moving documentary that chronicles the elusive search for happiness across multiple cultures. It includes the story of a man who lives in India. From any perspective, this man is living in squalor, but he is so full of love for his young son that he is a truly happy man.

And at the opposite end of the spectrum, don't you know people who have a lot of money who aren't happy? Who, no matter what, it's never enough?

Again, it's not your circumstances, it's how you react to your circumstances.

- How do you *think* about your circumstances?
- How do you *talk* about your circumstances?
- How do you *feel* about your circumstances?

In each chapter of this book we're going to focus on a different area of your life. I'm going to share how things happened in my life to get me to see and understand and feel and totally know that Nothing Is Wrong. Then, I'm going to give you a process. It's what I call a **Stepping Stone** (as we're on the *Journey* to Happy), and each one will help you in each area of your life to start moving out of the energy of Everything Is Wrong and into the energy of Nothing Is Wrong.

If you haven't already, watch my video
"Embracing the Concept of Nothing Is Wrong"

or go to: http://thejourneytohappy.com/video1/

Using the Stepping Stones on the Journey to Happy

Stepping Stone #1 – What's Your Story?

This is the beginning of the Find Out phase. What's your story? What do you tell yourself is wrong? What are the thoughts you think over and over again that tell you that specific things in your life aren't okay?

It might seem somewhat contradictory that I'm saying that Nothing Is Wrong while I'm also encouraging you to list out everything you think is "wrong" in your life. This book is all about self-awareness. One of the most important things we can do is to bring our thoughts into conscious awareness. The first step to healing is knowing and understanding what needs to be healed. We can't ignore it or run away from it. We can't pretend that it's not there. We can't stuff it down. All of these pointless attempts just make it worse and worse. By bringing up what we think is wrong, we can bring it into the light for healing. Very often, as we start thinking or writing about one thing, other things that are in our subconscious will start popping up.

The part that is interesting to me is the definition of the word "story". Merriam-Webster defines it as "an account of real *or imaginary* people and events". I'm not saying that your story isn't true, but isn't it interesting how it can change? Isn't it fascinating how something happening to one person can have a devastating effect, but the same thing happening to another person won't affect them at all?

Stepping Stone #1 is a quick but powerful exercise. It's a building exercise, so it's important that you do this. **Take ten minutes** and list in your journal everything you can think of that is wrong with every area of your life. For example, write everything that you don't like about your body. For me it was that I was 40 pounds overweight, my waist was too big, I couldn't wear the clothes I wanted, etc. Don't write paragraphs; quickly list words and phrases so that you can come back to it later and keep adding to it as more things come into your conscious awareness.

We'll call this your *Awareness List* because that is the most important aspect of this list – bringing all of the issues into your conscious awareness so that they can be healed.

Here are some prompts to help you:

What Is Wrong with:

- My Life?
- My Body?
- My Financial Situation?
- My Relationships (spouse or partner, children, family, friends, co-workers)?
- My Job, Work, or Career?
- The World in General?

Now that you've done this, we'll start unlocking the secrets of how to get out from under it.

You see, **the very things that we think are wrong are what we bring into our lives for healing.** So, not only is it not wrong, but it's also completely perfect. I'll say that again because it's *critical*. *The very things that we think are wrong are what we bring into our lives for healing.* They are the catalysts for growth.

We'll cover this in detail in the next chapter, but for now, take one more look at the Awareness List you've created, and then put it away.

What if there really IS something that appears to be wrong – I have an illness, my marriage is ending, I'm about to lose my house?

Please know that I'm not making light of your difficulties. Having experienced many challenges of my own (as you'll read about), I have deep compassion for where you are, BUT I also know that there is a way out! The famed speaker Zig Ziglar once said, "It's not what happens to you that matters. It's how you respond to what happens to you that makes all the difference." In these pages, I hope to give you some tools and insights that can make all the difference.

I'm NOT saying that everything is perfect, that everything is wonderful, or that everything is exactly the way you want it. What I AM saying is that staying in the energy of Everything Is Wrong will continue to make you stay stuck. I stayed stuck in all areas of my life until I learned the principles in this book and then finally started to really understand them and apply the idea that Nothing Is Wrong, and things didn't start to change until I actually experienced it. More on that in the next chapter.

I talk a lot about this topic in my weekly Sedona Soul Adventures email newsletter. If you'd like to receive it (it's free), we'll send it to you.

or go to: https://SoulAdventures.Infusionsoft.com/app/form/ JourneyToHappy

CHAPTER II

NOTHING IS WRONG WITH ME
Learning to Love Yourself

My life changed when I finally learned this and implemented it. My work, my body, my relationship with myself, my relationship to everyone else, my finances, my beautiful home, and (most importantly) my ability to live a happier and more peaceful life all came from this realization.

Have You Ever Asked Yourself, *"What's Wrong With Me?"*

I think most of us feel like we're a little different from everyone else and maybe even a little strange. Haven't there been times when you've said to yourself, "What's wrong with me?"

But the truth is, there is nothing wrong with you, and there is nothing wrong with me.

Our problems come from our *reactions* to what's going on. We cause ourselves grief, upset, unrest, and dissatisfaction by agonizing over circumstances that we don't prefer.

Everything that happens just *is*. It's energy moving in a particular way. It's when we judge and characterize something as wrong that we create all of the problems in our lives.

The Day I "Got It" That Nothing Is Wrong

I started on my spiritual path during one of the lowest times of my life. My mother, who had suffered for over five years with cancer, had died at the age of 51 (I was 26). I was depressed and angry.

I was angry with God. If anyone had told me at that moment that "Nothing Is Wrong" or "Everything is happening for a reason," I would have smacked them in the face!

The doctors sent my mother home at Christmas. This was at a time before hospice care had been established in the Midwest, and my father had no idea how to take care of her. I was away at law school and came home for Christmas. It was the worst Christmas of my entire life.

I came home again in late January. I'd decided that I wanted to have The Big Talk with my mother and tell her that I loved her and that I was sorry for anything I had ever done to hurt or disappoint her.

Of course, what I really wanted was for my mother to tell me that she loved me – to actually say the words. In our very German-American family, no one ever said that to each other. My mother told me that she loved me only once during a phone conversation when she had been ill. She'd called to wish me a Happy Valentine's Day (which was strange, as our family didn't celebrate Valentine's Day except in school).

We'd talked on the phone about how she was feeling (not very well) and how college was going (fine), and then at the end she suddenly said, "I love you." I was so taken aback that I was speechless. I quickly said, "I love you, too," and got off the phone and started crying. I realized that Mother had never said those words to me before, and it felt so strange, so unfamiliar for her to be saying them now. I realized that it was so unfamiliar that it actually made me feel uncomfortable.

Four years later, I went home in January hoping that I could get Mother to say those words again. But when I got there, she was so out of it from her pain and medication that I knew we wouldn't be able to have a real conversation. And because people were around her constantly, I didn't feel I could speak freely to her. She died ten days later. I was devastated.

One month after Mother's death, as I was driving to a law school class, I listened to a psychic on a morning radio show. The psychic was spot on in her readings with various guests. Something about it stuck with me. Though I had never done anything like it before, I called in and made an appointment for a reading.

She said that Mom was in a much better place; that she had been completely depleted in life, but that she had regained her soul and was happy to be out of pain and in spirit. I found that very comforting.

I told her that I was worried about my dad who had not handled mom's death well. She said, "He's very sad and feeling very guilty, but there's someone helping him who loves him and he cares deeply for her. She's a large woman with dark hair and her name starts with 'M'."

"That's Mary," I said, "but she's just a family friend. They don't have a romantic relationship." That's what I believed because that's what my parents told us.

The psychic, an older woman who seemed very wise said, "Well, there is a relationship between them." I kept up the "party line" and kept telling her that she was wrong; my dad and Mary were only friends, etc., etc., etc., and this little silver haired lady looked at me and smiled sweetly and said, "There's sex there, Dear."

Then she paused before adding, "In fact, they're going to get married in September. It will be very sudden. He'll call you on the phone to invite you to the wedding."

I vehemently told her that wasn't possible and left thinking, "Why did I even do this when everyone knows psychics are just a bunch of bunk anyway?"

One month later I had lunch with my aunt (my mother's sister) who started talking to me as if I knew about this affair that had gone on for many, many years, but which my mother had never discussed with me.

And of course, in September I got the phone call from my dad saying, "Mary and I are getting married this weekend. Can you come home?"

The psychic had completely nailed it.

I became fascinated with spirituality. I read books about near-death experiences, learned about past lives and astrology, and began studying meditation. I started traditional therapy. I went to workshops. I received energy readings. Although much of it was still focused on trying to "fix" what was "wrong", looking back, I can see that I was inching my way toward peace.

Then one day some years later it happened – completely out of the blue. My (then) husband and I had an argument. As usual, the argument transitioned to his belief that no matter what he had done or not done, there was never any justification for my being angry with him. The problem was never the issue that I was angry about. The problem was my anger and me. There was something wrong with *me*.

The fight struck something deep. I went home, alone. I began sobbing and sobbing and sobbing. Finally, I was sobbing so hard that I just climbed into bed.

All of a sudden, my body started vibrating. It was vibrating so much that I couldn't move. I just lay there and breathed. Then I heard a voice in my head, saying, "Nothing is wrong with you." "Nothing is wrong with you." "Nothing is wrong with you." The voice repeated those words over and over.

I knew something important was happening. I knew I needed to hold onto this. It felt like this was something that was coming in through the grace of God.

And then I was being shown that nothing was wrong in all areas of my life – my personality, my career, my body – all areas with which I had struggled. I simply *got it* that things were fine just the way they were. In an instant, I saw my entire life in a new way.

I saw how desperately I had been trying to change myself and how even the "spiritual" work that I'd been pursuing was about shaping myself into a different person as opposed to connecting with Spirit. My focus wasn't on trying to connect with God; my focus was on trying to be a different person. I thought that was the way to be "spiritual". I thought I had to be different so that my husband (and everyone else) would love me. I realized that I had believed that the only way that I could be loved was by becoming someone else, because deep down inside I hadn't believed that I was worthy of love.

And at that moment, I realized how wrong I'd been.

When my husband came home from the office that night, I told him about my experience. He said, "Of course there's nothing wrong with you," but he then went on to add, "except that you get angry with me and you don't treat me the way you should." Another argument started brewing.

Somehow, I had the presence of mind to stop the argument. At that moment, I understood that the only thing that was wrong was that *I thought something was wrong*. I wanted my husband to behave differently and to agree that nothing was wrong with me.

But he didn't have to agree.

There was nothing wrong with me, and I knew it, even if he didn't validate my newfound realization.

I woke up. I realized that the process begins with me. It revolutionized everything – and if you stick with me throughout the remainder of this book, you can have a similar experience.

Stepping Stone #2 – Change Your Story, Change Your Life

One of the powerful sessions that I facilitate at Sedona Soul Adventures is called "Change Your Story, Change Your Life". When we design customized retreats for our clients, we spend a considerable amount of time talking to them, before they come to Sedona, about what's happening in their lives and what transformations they most desire. Often during these discovery sessions, we can tell that some people are so badly hurting and they're so invested in their story of what's wrong with them (or their spouse if it's a couple's retreat) that there is no room for thinking of anything else. Even when we ask them to imagine that they could wave a magic wand and have everything the way they want it to be, they can't respond. They remain fixated on what's wrong with everything and everybody else. That's when we have them do my session, "Change Your Story, Change Your Life."

It's simple – but not easy. This is the basic concept of Change Your Story, Change Your Life: **if you stop thinking and talking about what you *don't* want and start focusing on and talking about what you *do* want, the energy shifts and amazing things can happen.**

Monitor your speech and keep track of how often you talk about things that are "wrong". Mark it down in your journal. You don't have to write down what you said or what the topic was. You can just draw a line for each occurrence.

I'm not talking about a situation in your work that requires you to address a problem. I'm talking about how often you start or continue a conversation related to things that aren't okay with you – the weather, the government, traffic, your spouse, your children, your in-laws, your extended family, your boss, your employees, your co-workers, your aches and pains, the line at Starbucks, etc. If you're meticulous with your journal entries and mark each occurrence down, you will probably be amazed and humbled and embarrassed.

I did a "Change Your Story, Change Your Life" session a few years ago with a woman who was completely astounded by the power of this concept. She felt the energy of all of the negative words she had been saying over the years. Right then and there, she made a vow to stop talking about how awful her husband was. This simple change completely revolutionized her marriage!

If you're feeling really adventurous, in addition to NOT talking about what's wrong, you might start actively talking about things that you like or things that you appreciate.

There is always something to appreciate, even if it's just that you're alive – and how fantastic is it that you're alive?

If you haven't already, watch my video "Get Happy Right Now (*Change Your Story, Change Your Life*)"

or go to: http://thejourneytohappy.com/video2/

Using the Stepping Stones on the Journey to Happy

Stepping Stone #1 – What's Your Story?

Has reading this chapter made you think of even more things that are wrong? Again, it may sound contradictory for me to say it, but that's great! The deeper we go, the more things will come up for healing. If there are more things to add to your Awareness List of things that are wrong, go ahead and add them now. Don't be discouraged. It's a good thing! Ironically, more often than not when I actually say out loud (or write in my journal) what I "think" is wrong, I can see almost immediately that not only is it not wrong, but it's actually perfect. The only thing that's wrong is my wrong-headed thinking. It's not what's going on; it's my reaction to what's going on.

I'm NOT saying that you don't have problems and pressures and that you haven't had things happen to you that have affected you. What I AM saying is that for most people, the majority of our problems come from our resistance to what is going on. If something that is happening is not to our preference, we cause ourselves more grief, more upset, more unrest, and more dissatisfaction by continuing to agonize over it.

It is when we go into judgment – when we characterize something as wrong – that we create most of the problems in our lives.

What if there really IS something that appears to be wrong with me – I'm mean, I'm depressed, I'm not successful enough, I'm not good looking, etc., etc., etc.?

This is exactly what I'm talking about! At some point, you simply have to find a way to stop all of the self-criticism and start to do the things that can bring you into the energy of loving yourself. It's not something you can do in just a day, but it starts with that basic decision. As the Buddha said, "You yourself, as much as anybody in the entire Universe, deserve your love and affection." Are you going to argue with Buddha?

Every religious tradition teaches that God loves us. If God loves you, isn't it time for you to start loving you? Read on and we'll delve into this more deeply.

CHAPTER III

NOTHING IS WRONG WITH YOU
(OR ANYONE ELSE)
Learning to Love Everyone

Have You Ever Asked Yourself, *"Why Do I Feel So Different From Everyone Else?"*

In the last chapter, we established my belief that Nothing Is Wrong with me.

We're now going to establish that Nothing Is Wrong with you (or anyone else).

One of the first things that I want you to say to yourself is, **"Nothing is wrong with me!"** Close your eyes, take a deep breath, and say out loud, "Nothing is wrong with me, nothing is wrong with me, nothing is wrong with me."

This might feel uncomfortable – even like a lie at this point – but it's the beginning.

It will help us come to the profound truth that if nothing is wrong with us, nothing is wrong with those around us, either.

One of the first things that I want to tell you about yourself is that whatever is going on with you regarding who you are as a person, it is something for which you are already wired. That won't make sense right now, but stay with me for a moment.

In my own quest for achieving such awareness, one of the most important things for me was to reach at least a level of self-awareness about who I am and who I *really* am. To that end, for over 30 years I have participated in an enormous amount of traditional therapy (15 years), counseling sessions, and couple's therapy. From the time I started on my spiritual path (and continuing to this day), I've had a vast number of psychic readings, Angel readings, Tarot readings, numerology readings, channeling sessions, Western astrology readings, Vedic astrology readings, Shamanic astrology readings, past life readings, chakra readings, etc., etc. In my opinion, these experiences have been incredibly valuable. I don't believe that we are bound by this information, but I believe that it gives us the knowledge to transcend it and utilize the insights to stay on the right course.

These are some of the sessions that we offer (when it's appropriate) as part of our Sedona Soul Adventures retreats, and I must tell you that the practitioners here in Sedona are so phenomenally gifted at applying their knowledge and expertise and have helped me understand and navigate so many issues in my life over the past 17 years. One of the information gathering processes that has been the most valuable for me over the years (and one that you can easily access on your own) is the Enneagram. I'd like to introduce that to you now.

The Enneagram – the Ultimate Key to Your Personality

The Enneagram originated in the Middle East several hundred years ago and was brought to the West by the Crusaders. Because monks kept the process alive during the Dark Ages, many Roman Catholics are aware of the Enneagram.

The Enneagram is a system for deeply understanding your basic personality that consists of a simple test. Results are revealed in a numbered system from one to nine (that I prefer to call "Styles"). It helps you understand what makes you tick and what is driving you. It can also help you to see what makes other people tick and what's driving them.

This information is vital because it tells you how you are wired. It helps you see that some of your quirks and patterns are a deep part of who you are and that you don't necessarily choose them. It doesn't mean that you don't accept responsibility – quite the contrary. By taking total responsibility, you can take this information and use it for transformation.

Each Style represents a deep belief that an individual uses to help navigate their life, but these beliefs are actually lies that are holding the self back from a connection with happiness, love, and contentment. You aren't telling yourself this lie consciously; it's an unconscious belief that is usually buried very deeply. When you discover the lies that you are telling yourself, it's as though the entire world opens up. When you discover the lies other people tell themselves, it brings you to a deep level of understanding and compassion for them.

When you are still operating your life based on a lie, you are operating as your unhealed self. Once you see the truth, you can move toward healing.

In an interesting book I read about the Enneagram, the author said that there is an "initial shock" in finding out exactly who you are – and he's exactly right. It was a shock to find out not only how I do things but to also discover how other people do things.

When observing human interactions, something I see all of the time is how almost everyone assumes that others will react in the same way that they do to a particular situation.

Nothing could be further from the truth. In a small group that we organized around the Enneagram in Sedona, we made a point to talk about particular situations and our individual reactions to them. I was stunned to discover how differently people responded. A situation that would make me incredibly angry, for example, would be absolutely no problem for someone else.

Understanding Your Style

Listed below are very brief synopses of each Style. Each explanation will start with the Lies (the unconscious beliefs that keep us out of connection) that people with different Styles tell themselves. Then, characteristics that are at the extremes of both spectrums will be listed as either healed or unhealed. Please keep in mind that no one that I know is completely healed or unhealed.

There are wonderful qualities about each Style, and there are qualities that each Style wants to heal, which is why I am using these terms. I don't use them as blame or judgment because, of course, Nothing Is Wrong with any of the Numbers or Styles. It's just the way that we're all wired to navigate the world.

Please understand that I don't consider myself an expert on the Enneagram. Although I have studied it for many years, this is not a book about the Enneagram. I include it here as an introduction to encourage you to start looking at the basic information within the Enneagram to unlock deeper understanding and compassion for yourself and others.

- **Style One – The Perfectionist**

"Everything has to be perfect for me to be happy."

Unhealed Ones are: critical, controlling, anxious

Healed Ones are: ethical, honest, high-principled, ambitious

- **Style Two – The Helper**

"I have to do things for people for them to love me."

<u>Unhealed Twos are</u>: passive aggressive, possessive, manipulative, irrational

<u>Healed Twos are</u>: warm, loving, caring, giving, adaptable

- **Style Three – The Achiever**

"I must work hard, do well, and look good to be happy."

<u>Unhealed Threes are</u>: driven, dishonest, pretentious, vain, consumed by what others think about them

<u>Healed Threes are</u>: optimistic, efficient, energetic, practical

- **Style Four – The Romantic Adventurer**

"I must be different and special to matter."

<u>Unhealed Fours are</u>: depressed, moody, self-absorbed, temperamental

<u>Healed Fours are</u>: romantic, expressive, supportive, compassionate

- **Style Five – The Investigator**

"I must know everything about everything."

<u>Unhealed Fives are</u>: stubborn, negative, secretive, distant, arrogant about what they know

<u>Healed Fives are</u>: independent, inventive, wise, perceptive

- **Style Six – The Loyalist**

"By being loyal to someone or something else, I will be taken care of."

<u>Unhealed Sixes are</u>: anxious, controlling, paranoid, insecure

<u>Healed Sixes are</u>: loyal, practical, responsible, self-reliant, team players

- **Style Seven – The Enthusiast**

"I must avoid pain to be happy."

Unhealed Sevens are: possessive, manic, restive, narcissistic, scattered

Healed Sevens are: spontaneous, versatile, enthusiastic

- **Style Eight – The Aggressor**

"I have to fight for everything I have."

Unhealed Eights are: angry, aggressive, confrontational, grudge holders, think they are right about everything

Healed Eights are: courageous, direct, self-reliant, self-confident, decisive

- **Style Nine – The Peacemaker**

"I must have peace at any price."

Unhealed Nines are: stubborn, obsessive, judgmental, complacent, passive-aggressive, defensive

Healed Nines are: creative, accepting, trusting, supportive

Discovering That Nothing Is Wrong with My Anger – How I Went from Being an Unhappy Eight and Stopped Fighting with Everyone

I am an Eight on the Enneagram. Eights are the Fighters.

The big lie that Eights tell themselves is, "Life is hard. I have to work all my life, and then I'll die. I have to do everything by myself. There's no one to help. I have to fight for everything I have."

Could that be any more depressing or any more rooted in the belief that Everything Is Wrong?

Eights are naturally wired to fight. Whereas Nines have no boundaries, Eights are the experts at boundaries. Whatever you do, don't bump up against an (unhealed) Eight's boundaries, or you'll be sorry. Eights are very good at fighting the "good" fight, so it was very natural that I was politically active as a young person and fighting for women and children when I was an attorney, but mainly, I'm just wired to fight.

As I've mentioned, this was a major sticking point with my ex-husband Tom. Tom is a Nine ("peace at any price"), so the bulk of our arguments were about my anger. No matter what had happened, he was upset that I was upset, and our arguments usually revolved around whether or not my response was "okay". Of course, it never was because it was an angry response, so we almost never ended up discussing the issue at hand. We were always just arguing that it wasn't okay that I was angry.

What was worse was that I bought into the idea that my anger *wasn't* okay and that something was "wrong" with my anger. Therefore, something was wrong with me.

By this time in my life, I wanted to be a "spiritual person". Somehow I had bought into the idea that being a "spiritual person" meant being sweet and compliant and never getting angry. That I should be trying to act like a Goddess all of the time and speaking in a breathy voice, saying things like, "That's so beautiful." I never did any of that because I knew it would be completely phony – but I aspired to it.

I didn't want to get angry.
I didn't want to lose my temper.

Ironically, this was at the same time that I was becoming well-known as a divorce attorney. People would call me on the phone and say, "I hear you're a real bitch. I want you to be my lawyer." They actually meant it as a total compliment.

When I finally found out about the Enneagram, I felt a kind of liberation. The anger was not bad; it was a life force. It had enabled me to survive a rough childhood, to build inner strength, to take care of myself, and on and on. I began to view my anger as an asset, not a weakness or something to be ashamed of. I worked on ways to modulate my anger so that I wasn't spewing it out all over everyone all of the time, but I also stopped trying to shove it down. I stopped being ashamed of it, and I stopped hating myself when I got angry.

The power of the Enneagram is that it shows you where you are in disconnection and how you can bring yourself back into connection. **And, even in disconnection, we are perfection.**

That seems like a contradiction, but it's not.

The bottom line is that you are a beloved child of God *exactly the way that you are.*

You are wired to be the way that you are. If there is something that is causing you some pain, you can find it, understand it, and do something about it. You can love yourself back into connection.

But even before you do that, even with all of your wounds and scars and unhealed pain, *YOU ARE EXACTLY OKAY THE WAY THAT YOU ARE, RIGHT NOW, THIS MINUTE.*

Stepping Stone #3 – Take the Enneagram Test and Discover How You're "Wired" to Be the Way You Are

I want you to take this test now because it is a wonderful way to gain compassion for yourself. There are no good numbers and no bad numbers. Nothing Is Wrong with any of the numbers. This knowledge can bring you into conscious awareness of who you are.

This is a free test. It is on an interesting web site called *Eclectic Energies* (and I very much appreciate Eclectic Energies and its founder, Ewald Berkers of the Netherlands, for allowing me to give you access to the test). One of the things I like about this test is that in addition to discovering what Style you are, it will also give you information about your wing. Your primary Style will be one number and you will have influences from one of the numbers directly next to your number (e.g., I am an Eight with a Seven wing).

VERY IMPORTANT: Take the test and answer the questions as if you were 25 years old. If you are older than that, think of how you were at 25. That will show you how you are wired. For example, when I was 25, I got angry about absolutely everything.

Use the Code to go on-line to take the test.

Or go to: https://www.eclecticenergies.com/enneagram/ dotest.php

It takes 10 minutes. Then, come back and we will continue...

Now, take your highest score. If two scores are very close, do a little bit of reading about each of the numbers, and it will become pretty clear which Style you are.

Please STOP HERE and take the test. It's vitally important. After you've received your results, read the brief synopsis below about each Style. In each of the next chapters, we continue to build on this information.

Have you taken it? Good. Then proceed.

Here is the basic information that will help you have more compassion for yourself and others.

- **Style 1 – The Perfectionist**

Stop demanding that everything must be perfect. Relax more. Feel more compassion for people. As I used to say to one of my coaching clients who is a One, "Finished is better than perfect." Stop using the word "should". Appreciate that you are one of those people who wants things done in the best way possible.

- **Style 2 – The Helper**

Stop doing the things that you don't want to do. If you truly want to do something for someone, do it without any expectation that they will return the favor. If that's okay with you, then proceed. Do things that really feel like splurges and take care of yourself (get massages and manicures, buy yourself flowers, take time out alone). Appreciate that you are full of love and genuinely want to help other people.

- **Style 3 – The Achiever**

Stop working to the point of exhaustion. Now is the time to be completely honest with other people and yourself. *What do you truly want?* Have you given up on your dreams? Don't be so concerned about what other people think of you. Stop buying things that you think will impress other people. Allow yourself to feel vulnerable. Appreciate that you are hardworking and dependable and that people are grateful for who you are.

- **Style 4 – The Romantic Adventurer**

When you start thinking that you are better than everyone else, stop it! Understand that everyone has dreams and desires. Focus less on the idea that other people don't understand you and instead make an effort to understand *them.* Create a morning exercise routine and then stick to it. Appreciate the fact that you are a very creative person and that you have a deep capability to connect with other people.

• Style 5 – The Investigator

Understand that, especially in this day and age, it's impossible to know everything about everything. Stop trying to prove that you know everything. Stop correcting people when you are in small groups (unless you are asked). Take up some kind of creative activity that will get you out of your head. Appreciate the fact that Albert Einstein was a Five, and you DO have an extraordinary mind.

• Style 6 – The Loyalist

Do things to counteract your pessimism and anxiety (physical exercise, meditation, reading inspirational books, music that makes you feel good, finding upbeat friends). Understand that we live in a world that tries to make us more anxious, so take yourself off the hook for the anxiety that you feel. Learn to cultivate trust in other people by first cultivating trust in yourself. Appreciate the fact that you are responsible and hardworking and loyal and can very often figure things out before other people do.

• Style 7 – The Enthusiast

Finish what you start. When you get up in the morning (or even better, at the end of the day before), make a list of two things to accomplish so that you always feel that you are getting things done. Realize that you don't have to do everything or have everything right now. Appreciate the fact that your basic disposition is one of happiness and optimism and that you are a generous person.

- **Style 8 – The Aggressor**

Stop fighting with everyone. Rush to give in even when you "know" you're right. Would you rather be right or would you rather be happy? Understand that not everyone is against you. Forgive slights by reminding yourself that most people are just doing the best they can with what they have. Don't be afraid to show the innate vulnerability and sweetness that you have within you. Appreciate the fact that you are strong and self-reliant and that you do what you say you will.

- **Style Nine – The Peacemaker**

Set boundaries. Understand that when there are conflicts, they need to be dealt with. Exercise or do other things to help you come more fully into your body. Do things that will help you to really feel and express your emotions. Stop spending so much time in front of television screens or computer screens. Appreciate the fact that you are open-minded, diplomatic, and receptive.

Regardless of your Style, embrace and utilize what you are wired for. After all, it's part of your life force! For me, it was about loving my anger and learning how I could use it for good. The really interesting thing was, once I figured that out, I gradually stopped getting angry with everyone.

Using the Stepping Stones on the Journey to Happy

Stepping Stone #1 – What's Your Story?

Now that you know what Style you are, has it brought up more items to add to your Awareness List? When I first read about myself (as an Eight), I was surprised (and embarrassed) to realize that I hold grudges and classify people as "loyal" or "disloyal". I assumed everyone did that!

If some more things have come up, add them to your list now, but do it in the spirit of "now that I'm aware of this, I can change it".

Stepping Stone #2 – Change Your Story, Change Your Life

Remember to refrain from talking about what's wrong with you or anyone else and start talking about things that you like about yourself (e.g., I'm funny, I'm responsible, I love my children).

I'm NOT saying that I don't ever get angry or upset anymore – I do. But I don't hate myself for it, and I don't keep trying to change my basic wiring. I'm not saying that the Enneagram has every single answer for what's going on with you, but just knowing that you're wired for certain things can help you begin to understand yourself and take yourself off the hook. That's where the philosophy of Nothing Is Wrong starts.

What if a person has broken the law or is abusive? Isn't that wrong?

In our discussion that Nothing Is Wrong, I'm not advocating that we go through life without boundaries or rules or laws. I was an attorney for 20 years, and I have a deep belief in the rule of law. People who have violated our beliefs of what is moral or ethical (murder, rape, violence, theft, etc.) are to be held accountable, and their actions are not to be condoned. However, I would hasten to add the admonishment from the Bible "judge not, lest ye be judged" and Christ's teaching to "love thy neighbor as thyself".

All religious traditions tell us to treat our fellow man with kindness and compassion. We can never know why bad things happen to good people.

We can never know if there is a Divine plan behind everything. My hope is that there is, and I take peace in believing that to be true.

I believe that we are all created in the image of God and that it is in our disconnection from Source that bad things happen. More on that later.

Now, let's start looking at specific areas of your Life.

CHAPTER IV

NOTHING IS WRONG WITH YOUR LIFE
Learning to Love Your Life

Have You Ever Looked at the People Around You and Asked, *"Why Is Everyone Else's Life So Much Better Than Mine?"*

The truth is, it isn't. Everyone's got his or her stuff going on.

Your life can get better pretty quickly when you shift the energy and start believing that Nothing Is Wrong with my life.

One of the truths that Einstein discovered (and that Quantum Physics continues to prove) is that everything is energy. Even the chair you're sitting in right now, which feels so stable and strong, is – at its core – just a bunch of particles racing around.

If everything is energy, that means that everything is much more elastic, much more malleable, and much more possible to change than we think it is.

We are sending out energy all of the time. The Institute of HeartMath has been studying this fact for the past 20 years, and one of the things they've found is that there is energy coming out of your heart center and projecting out about four feet. Scientists are now able to measure this. So, if energy is coming out of you all of the time, what kind of energy are you sending out?

Our Perceptions Determine How Our Lives Are

Think about all of the perceptions that have driven mankind's behaviors and caused us to do things that now seem very weird, silly, or just plain horrible.

For example:

- People believed for thousands of years that the earth was flat and that they would fall off if they went to the end of it.

- Religious scholars once taught and believed that the sun revolved around the Earth, a theory believed for many, many years. To believe or teach otherwise was considered heresy. Scientists were actually executed for teaching these theories. Galileo was nearly executed but instead remained under house arrest for the remainder of his life after he published the observations that he had made with his telescope that the Earth revolves around the sun.

- This is one of my favorite (crazy) ones. It was believed that you could determine who was a witch by throwing them in a river. If they were NOT a witch, they would sink (and most probably drown). If they floated, they were a witch, and you could then burn them at the stake!

- For years, no one believed that it was possible for a human being to run a mile in less than four minutes. There was so much written about it that it was believed to be empirically true by scientists and medical doctors. Then, Roger Bannister did it in 1954. Once it had been done, our mindset changed. More and more people did it, and the record has now been lowered by over 17 seconds. (It's also interesting to me that way back in 1954, Roger Bannister used visualization as part of his training).

Henry Ford said, "There are two kinds of people in the world – those who think they can and those who think they can't. And they're both right!"

That is so completely true! The way that I'm writing about all of this may sound like far-out woo-woo to some, but I prefer to call it "True WOO". You don't have to believe it for it to be true.

Look at successful people. I love reading biographies, and I can tell you that the people who are the most successful are those who believe that they are determining their own destiny. Said another way, successful people believe that they are creating their own reality. They don't listen when someone tells them it's impossible. They see opportunity where most other people see failure.

One of my favorite stories is about Thomas Edison. In his quest to invent an electric light bulb, he had over 700 "failed" experiments. A newspaper reporter asked Edison the question, "How does it feel to have failed 700 times?"

Edison famously replied, "I have not failed 700 times. I have not failed once. I have succeeded in proving that those 700 ways will not work. When I have eliminated all of the ways that will not work, I will find the way that will work."

One of my brothers (whom I love very much) is an atheist, but there isn't a person on the planet who believes more in the power of positive thinking. He might not call it exactly that, but he lives it, teaches it, and has spent hours and hours reading books and listening to self-development teachings. As far as I'm concerned, it's all the same thing.

The most beautiful thing is that he taught all of this to his wonderful son. From the time his son was a tiny baby, my brother told him that he could be anything he wanted to be, and that is exactly what happened. My nephew is an amazing physician, husband, father, and person. He's the whole package, and I know that a huge part of his accomplishments is because from day one he was encouraged to be or do or have whatever he wanted.

You are a beloved child of God, made in God's image, and loved by God. I don't care if you're a Hindu, Christian, Muslim, Jew, or Buddhist – every religion teaches this in one form or another.

And, even if you're an atheist, do you believe that there is some force or power in the Universe that is real and palpable?

We all have a spark of the Divine within us. It is that Divine connection that we can utilize to bring in the energy of Nothing Is Wrong and then manifest the peace and joy and happiness that we want.

We are energy, our thoughts are energy, and our emotions certainly result in energy.

We get more of whatever it is that we think about.

What we focus on expands.

Quantum Physics has proven that putting attention on something in any way changes it. The result of doing so is that we are all creating our reality in every moment.

That is great news! If you are creating your reality, that means that you can change the parts that you don't like – the parts that aren't making you happy.

If you are willing to take responsibility for creating your reality, then you can take responsibility for creating it the way you want it, and you can utilize that Divine connection – that spark of the Divine that is in every one of us, including you.

What Happened to My Divine Connection?

If you are reading this and are in a place in your life right now where everything seems to be wrong, let me tell you that I feel your pain. That's exactly where I was in January 1999 when I first came to Sedona. Every area of my life was messed up – work, marriage, money, body. I know how awful it is. I know what it feels like to not want to drag yourself out of bed to face another day.

What happened to your Divine Connection? I think of the Divine Connection as a beautiful jewel that resides within us and is strong and fantastic and perfect. But through the course of our lives, mud and dirt get splattered on it until it gets buried so deeply that we don't even realize that it's there anymore. All we can see and feel is the mud and dirt. We lose that connection to the Divine, and that feels really awful. It's in that disconnected state that people can do some pretty terrible things.

Have you heard the story about the golden statue in the Asian monastery? I don't know if it's true or just a teaching that I've heard many times, but I love this story. During a war, the monks knew that their monastery was about to be invaded. They had a large, beautiful statue of the Buddha made entirely of pure gold. They decided that to save the statue they would cover it over with mud and make it look like a simple ceramic statue. Many years passed, and after a few generations, everyone completely forgot that the statue was made of gold. One day the statue was being moved and the stucco cracked. Underneath was the beautiful brilliant gold!

I especially love two things about this story. The primary one is that the "real" Buddha, the golden Buddha (like the real [golden] you), is hidden underneath all of the gunk. The other part is that it takes a crack in the exterior coat of gunk for the real you to burst forth and be seen.

The trials and tribulations we all experience are just a set up for the cracking to take place. I had to reach my lowest point before I started to crack. Alcoholics Anonymous talks about hitting "rock bottom" before addicts are willing to do something to heal their addiction. The Bible talks about God being able to more easily come through "the cracked vessel".

How do mud and gunk get all over the jewel (the pure gold) that represents the true you? It happens in lots of ways, especially resulting from parents and teachers who had an impact on us when we were young and impressionable. Unknowingly, we take on their beliefs and ideas. When I first started what would become 15 years of therapy, I was astounded to find out how my life was mirroring that of my parents. My therapist encouraged me to look at the different areas of my life and compare them to how my parents' lives were in the same areas. I assured her there would be no similarities, as I was so different from my parents. What a revelation!

I looked at the big areas in my life. Here were my answers at the time:

Mom and Dad	Me
Life: Life is hard	Life is hard
Spirituality: Believed in God	Believe in a Higher Power
Work: You have to work really hard and do things you don't like to make money and support yourself.	I was working really hard and doing things I didn't like (practicing law) to make money and support myself.
Money: Made a lot of money. Spent a lot of money. There was never enough. Mother would sit at the dining room table and write out checks to pay bills and say, "There's not enough!"	Made a lot of money. Spent a lot of money. Never enough. Amazingly, I would also sit at the dining room table and write out checks to pay bills and say, "There's not enough!"
Relationships: Marriage is hard. Parents are distant. Father is working nights and completely unavailable.	I was already divorced by this time. I kept finding unavailable men. My first boyfriend was away at college. My first husband was in law school and studying all the time. My second husband was from Holland, and we had a long distance relationship until we got married. After that marriage ended, I had a relationship with an American who lived in Tokyo!
Body: My mother was constantly dieting, and as my father aged he became morbidly obese. He would go on diets and lose 30-40 pounds and then would go off the diet and gain it all back and more.	I was put on my first diet when I was 12, even though I wasn't fat. I would continually go on diets and lose 20 pounds, and then I would go off the diet and gain it all back and more.

Although I thought I was completely different from my parents, I was completely like them in terms of how everything in my life was manifesting. When I realized that I was even sitting at the dining room table writing out checks to pay bills and saying, "There's not enough," I was totally, completely stunned. These patterns are set in ways that we don't even realize until we start to consciously look at them.

Stepping Stone #4 – Discover the Patterns That You Took On as a Child That are Affecting You to This Day

Take ten minutes to think about how your parents, teachers, or others (who really influenced you as a child) interacted with the world. For most people, it will be your parents. How did they "do" money? How did they "do" food? How did they "do" relationships?

Remember, this is not about blame; this is about raising your conscious awareness. As I've said, we are creating our reality in every moment. I know I created these parents and I created these patterns. This is not my parents' fault. I chose (unconsciously) to take on their thoughts and perceptions. This was one of the most valuable processes I ever did in my life, so I invite you to do it now.

Write down how your parents thought about various areas in their lives and how it showed up in their lives. If there was a teacher or another influential person in your life, you can substitute them. Then, list the answers for what *you* think and how this is showing up in *your* life.

Parents/Guardians/Teachers	**Me**

General Attitude or Thinking about:

1. Life
2. Work
3. Money
4. Body/Food/Health
5. Relationships
6. Spirituality
7. The State of the World

What to Do with This Information

Now that you see the patterns, what do you do? How do you stop blowing through money or jumping from one unhappy relationship to another? My former therapist and many teachers seem to think that simply the awareness of these things is enough to change them.

I don't agree. After 30 years of reading a zillion books, undergoing therapy, and going to hundreds of workshops and seminars where it was nothing but talk, talk, talk, I have come to believe that simple awareness is not enough. Something needs to *actually happen* to Clear Out the mud and gunk and uncover the jewel – the pure gold that is the real you.

Several years ago, I discovered Breathwork and other types of energy work that are designed to move this energy up and out. We do these processes here at Sedona Soul Adventures, and that's why the retreats are so transformational. But there are also simple things that you can do on your own. We'll talk about some of them in the next chapter as we drill down into more specifics – your body, your money, your relationships.

Of course, now that you have gained this awareness, there are steps that you can take immediately. For me, one of the first things I did was to stop writing checks at the dining room table! I also broke up with the guy in Tokyo. Here are some things that you can do right now:

Using the Stepping Stones on the Journey to Happy

Stepping Stone #1 – What's Your Story?

Now that you've completed this process, incorporate the patterns that you took on from your parents that are no longer serving you and add them to your Awareness List.

Stepping Stone #2 – Change Your Story, Change Your Life

Stop talking about how your parents ruined your life. Start talking about what your parents did *for* you. You're alive, and they didn't kill you, right?

Stepping Stone #3 – The Enneagram Fit

From here on out, I'll be showing you how the Enneagram impacts each area of your life and how you can utilize the Enneagram to move the energy. While some of the statements below may sound simple, they contain insights that will broaden your awareness and understanding.

- **Style One – The Perfectionist**

  As a child, you were probably very critical of yourself, so the healing comes in stopping the self-criticism.

- **Style Two – The Helper**

  As a child, you probably exhibited dramatic or precocious behavior as a way to get attention. Healing comes when you stop doing things to get attention and stop agreeing to do things that you don't want to do just to receive love.

- **Style Three – The Achiever**

  As a child, you probably told little white lies to avoid getting into trouble or to look good in front of parents and teachers. The healing comes when you decide to always tell the truth even concerning so-called "little" things.

- **Style Four – The Romantic Adventurer**

  As a child, you probably didn't get along with your parents and may still feel estranged. Healing comes from taking some steps to mend that relationship, especially through forgiveness.

- **Style Five – The Investigator**

  As a child, you probably spent a lot of time alone reading books or involved in other solitary activities. Healing comes through spending less time alone and interacting more with other people.

- **Style Six – The Loyalist**

  As a child, you probably took on feelings of anxiety from a dysfunctional parent or situation. Healing comes from examining that and taking steps to move through it.

- **Style Seven – The Enthusiast**

  As a child, you probably spent a lot of time daydreaming about a lot of different things. Healing comes from staying focused on one thing at a time.

- **Style Eight – The Aggressor**

  Most Eights grew up before their time and were little adults at a young age. Healing comes from becoming more playful.

- **Style Nine – The Peacemaker**

  As a child, you probably "tuned out" a lot, especially during household conflicts. Healing comes from facing unpleasantness head on and establishing (and maintaining) boundaries.

I'm NOT saying that you didn't have a difficult childhood and that it couldn't have been better. What I AM saying is that one of the most powerful steps in this process is to take back your power and decide that you are going to stop blaming your parents or teachers or the way that you were raised or the things that happened to you for what's "wrong" with you. The simple path to happiness is to let go of that baggage. Nearly everybody has experienced a difficult childhood or difficult problems. Talk about it. Perhaps you can engage in therapy or a retreat to work through it. Cry about it.

And now...*Enough!*

Make the decision that you are no longer going to allow these people or events to assume control over you, because that is the real key here. As long as you allow the pain to continue (especially over something that happened 10 or 20 years ago), those who hurt you win. Forgive your parents. Understand that they were doing their best with the limited skills that they had. Understand their behaviors probably stemmed from pain that you don't even know about or completely comprehend. Don't forgive them as a favor to them. Forgive them as a favor to yourself – to lift that energy once and for all!

I realize more than anyone that it's very easy for me to tell you to just "stop" doing this. I know that it will take time. But believe me, simply making the decision to *try* to stop and to *try* to forgive is incredibly powerful in itself, and it starts the process.

What if something really terrible HAS happened to me in my life?

Every day, incomprehensible things happen – children die, people are wrongly imprisoned, a natural disaster kills thousands of people. We can allow these things to destroy us; that is certainly a choice that we have. I love the quote from Nelson Mandela (who was imprisoned for 37 years), "As I walked out the door toward the gate that would lead to my freedom, I knew that if I didn't leave my bitterness and hatred behind, I'd still be in prison." We can keep ourselves in prison, or we can give ourselves the freedom that comes with peace. Mandela also said, "Forgive others, not because they deserve forgiveness, but because you deserve peace."

Who do you need to forgive? God? Yourself? Someone else? It may take more than a simple decision like the one Nelson Mandela made, but there is peace on the other side of that decision.

In the next chapter, we're going to work on something that took me many years to finally get handled. Don't wait as long as I did to get happy with your body!

CHAPTER V

NOTHING IS WRONG WITH YOUR BODY
Loving Your Body

Have You Ever Asked Yourself, *"Why Does Even Looking at Food Make Me Gain Weight?"*

It's due to how you're thinking about it and how you are feeling about it.

So let's recap.

Everything is energy.

You are creating your reality in every moment (whether you believe it or not).

You are sending out energy and vibrations in every moment.

Thoughts are things. Quantum Physicists are proving that even focusing attention on something changes it.

When we think about something, we get more of it. If we're worried about something, we bring it faster. If we're excited about something, we bring it faster.

What we resist persists. What we fight gets bigger and bigger because we are pouring more and more energy into whatever it is that we are fighting.

When we allow ourselves to, we move into the energy of All That Is. We move into the energy of All Possibilities. From that place, you can discover almost magical possibilities.

Our thoughts bring on our emotions.

Our Emotions Are the Most Powerful Tools That We Can Use for Finding Our Way to Happiness

In every moment, our emotions are telling us how we're feeling, how we're flowing energy, and how we're vibrating.

Although these ideas may seem complicated, they're really very simple. We are either feeling good, or we are feeling bad. It's pretty much as simple as that. We have all of these names for emotions. We have ones that have been labeled "good" – happiness, joy, bliss, contentment, or peace – and we have ones that have been labeled "bad" – anger, depression, frustration, rage, worry, anxiety, ennui, or despondency.

In every moment, we have the ability to move toward good feelings or bad feelings. Good feelings move us into energetic vibrations that bring us the things we want – happiness, contentment, peace, and joy. Negative feelings take us in the opposite direction.

Our physical bodies are the most perfect and precise examples of this energy in action. Take a moment right now to think about how you feel about your body. Do you like it or do you dislike it? Are you happy with it or do you constantly wish it would be different?

This is an area of struggle for so many people. I struggled with it for over 40 years. Of course, it's a big thing because our bodies are with us 24/7. We can never get away from them. But one thing that we can do – that we have control over – is how we think and feel about our bodies.

How I Went from a Size 14 to a Size 6 and Lost 40 Pounds by NOT Dieting...and Now Eat and Drink Whatever I Want Whenever I Want

I started thinking that something was wrong with my body at around the age of eight. I started ballet and tap lessons when I was three. I loved performing. I remember my first dance costume as if I could see it right now. We were performing a tap dance to *"I'm a Cowpoke from the Rio Grande"* and our costume was a short red felt skirt with gold fringe, a white cowboy shirt with big red polka dots, and a red felt cowboy hat. In ballet, I had the moves, but I didn't have the body. I'm short (5'4"), and I have a short waist and short torso – a far cry from the long legs, arms, and torso it takes to be a really extraordinary ballerina.

I remember receiving criticism about my body at the age of eight. I was put on my first diet at the age of 12. I look back at pictures of myself, and I wasn't fat.

All of this attention to my body started to take a toll. I wanted my body to be different. I wanted it to do things that it didn't do naturally.

All this focus on being told I was "fat" had an effect as well, mainly that I started to believe it. In high school, three different things happened. My hormones started really kicking in, my father's alcoholism really started manifesting, and my mother started working because of our suddenly serious financial situation.

All of a sudden we stopped having an evening meal together, and instead, we all fended for ourselves. Mother would make sure that there was food there, but we weren't sitting down to a meal unless it was Sunday. Suddenly I gained ten pounds. Horrified, I really started dieting in earnest.

I lost the ten pounds, but it came back almost immediately, and worse, it started an up-and-down yo-yo cycle that lasted continuously for over 30 years.

In college, I majored in theatre and dance. To get roles, I couldn't be overweight. I was constantly on a diet, and so was my husband. The cycle continued, except at that time we were gaining and losing 20 pounds over and over again.

I began to hate my body. I hated the constant struggle. I tried absolutely everything – Weight Watchers, Jenny Craig, NutriSystem, the grape diet, the Dolly Parton diet, the olive oil diet, the Stillman Diet, the Scarsdale diet, the Atkins diet, the Palm Beach diet, low carb, high protein, fasts, shakes – I've been vegetarian, vegan, and gone raw. I admit that there were even times that I resorted to bulimia. I have deep memories of how disgusted I was with myself after I had put my fingers down the back of my throat and made myself throw up after gorging on food.

I've purchased almost every piece of exercise equipment from small to large, used them, sold them, and bought another one. I've had personal trainers and have even lived in an apartment building above a health club and would get up at 5:30 a.m. five days per week to work out.

I've purchased over-the-counter pills and consumed apple cider vinegar. I've taken all types and combinations of vitamins and supplements designed to lose weight, boost metabolism, increase energy, etc. I tried prescription drugs, but they made me way too jumpy. At one point, I even started smoking cigarettes to kill my appetite.

I was completely obsessed.

It was always the same thing. I would be very disciplined for a while (for as much as six months at a time) and would lose

20-30 pounds. Then, the minute I even started thinking about eating "regular" food again, I would gain it all back and more.

I found a journal not too long ago in which I wrote, "75% of my unhappiness comes from my weight and my struggles with my body." Wow. How sad is that?

I actually told myself once that if I could find something (a procedure, a shot, a pill, anything) that would magically make my body be the weight I wanted it to be on a permanent basis, that I would do anything it took to make that happen. Even if it cost $20,000, I would mortgage my house, take out a loan – *anything* just to get rid of this constant weight problem dragging me down.

Every morning when I awoke, my first thoughts were about what and how I was going to eat that day. My mood for the day was set by the reading of the scale. If my weight was down, I started the day off in a good mood. If it was up, I was depressed and usually angry.

I had two complete sets of clothes – my fat clothes (size 12-14) and my other clothes (size 8-10).

When I think of the time and energy and money that I spent over the years related to losing weight, I'm convinced that I could have built the Empire State Building three times all by myself.

The worst part was that I was already learning from a number of teachers, books, and workshops that loving our bodies is the only way to have them be the way that we want them to be. I bought books and cassette tapes and CDs with meditations. I wrote Affirmations. I visualized how I wanted my body to be.

I had the vague idea that there was Nothing Wrong with my body, but I had no idea how to implement that knowing.

Suddenly, the event happened that I described in Chapter 2 when my body started vibrating and I "got it" that there is nothing wrong with me. Part of that was seeing, feeling, and understanding that there was nothing wrong with my body, either.

"Nothing is wrong with your body", "Nothing is wrong with your body", "Nothing is wrong with your body". That was a big one to swallow (pardon the pun).

Immediately, I made the decision to just stop. The obsession had to stop. I threw up my hands. I gave in. I surrendered. I decided to stop all dieting, stop thinking about food all of the time, and stop the obsessive exercising.

I figured that I was going to balloon up to 250 pounds. But that's not what happened.

At the same time, I was really incorporating all of the spiritual work that I had done, and I was utilizing the amazing practitioners at Sedona Soul Adventures. I did Breathwork and different types of emotional clearing. My focus became loving myself – not loving myself so that I could lose weight, but loving myself so that I could experience the contentment and peace it brings.

I stopped thinking about food. I stopped talking about food. Do you even realize how much people talk about food? I stopped working out obsessively. I did still go on hikes with my dog, but that was because I just loved being out in nature in Sedona, and I loved hiking with my dog.

I started eating what I wanted. I would check in with my body, and I would eat whatever I felt like eating. Sometimes that would be something really "healthy" like a green smoothie. Sometimes it would be an In 'n Out cheeseburger and, of course, fries and a chocolate shake! I started to find that it seemed like I was fuller faster. I ate until I wasn't hungry and very often left food on my plate because I was satisfied.

Before, if I gave myself permission to eat something, I would eat absolutely all of it and probably lick the plate. I went on one diet that said you could eat all the carbs you want for one hour each day before 7 p.m. As long as you ate carbs only during that one hour, you would lose weight. For me, low carb diets had always worked well for weight loss, so I tried it. If you had seen me design this binge hour, you would have thought that I was building a spacecraft, it was so intricate. I would literally stuff everything I wanted (cheeseburgers, pie, fried chicken, French fries, bread) into this hour. I would time it so that if we were going to a movie later, I could eat popcorn and coke and candy before the hour ended. I remember feeling so stuffed from the overeating. Unlike most of the other diets, I didn't lose any pounds. What a surprise!

Now, I started eating "devil carbs" whenever I wanted. The difference was that I didn't think of them as devil carbs. I just ate what I wanted when I wanted it, and I didn't worry or fret about it.

The most astonishing thing happened. The weight started melting off! It was over a period of fewer than two months. I didn't even realize it until I went shopping for a new pair of jeans. I tried on a size 14, and it was way too big! To my utter amazement, I was a size 6!

I decided to do a nutritional cleanse that was focused on health, not weight loss. In fact, I was told that weight gain sometimes occurs as a result of nutrient redistribution associated with the cleanse. But I didn't gain any weight, I even lost a few more pounds.

Before, I didn't think that I could be happy unless I became thin. Once I decided I could be happy without being thin, I became thin. Isn't that the craziest thing? I slimmed down from a size 14 to a size 6 and have stayed there for over five years.

Here is a before and after picture of me. The first one was taken when I started coming to Sedona in 2000. The other one is me now. And as you can see from the photo, I'm not skinny-model thin, I'm just not fat anymore.

(Left) This is how I looked when I first started coming to Sedona in 2000.

(Right) This is me standing in front of the very famous Cathedral Rock in Sedona, and no, this photo has not been changed or photo-shopped in any way. I really am standing in front of Cathedral Rock and that's what I look like.

I really knew that the body thing was handled once and for all when I went on one of our Sedona Soul Adventures trips to Bali. For every other trip that we ever took (to Egypt, Peru, or Bali), I would always go on a diet 60 days before the trip and lose 20-25 pounds. Then, I would go on the trip and eat and drink whatever I wanted because I wanted to enjoy the trip. During the trip, I would tell myself and everyone else how much weight I was gaining. By the time the two-week trip was over, I would come home and get on the scale and see what I already knew was going to happen. I'd gained back the 20 pounds, plus a little more.

This time, I went on the Bali trip and ate and drank whatever I wanted, including a chocolate croissant every morning (sometimes two!), along with my eggs and toast and potatoes and café latte and orange juice, because it all tasted so good and I loved it so much. I celebrated every single bite, and I never engaged in talk (or thoughts) about how fattening it was, etc. Instead, I just loved and enjoyed every single thing I put in my mouth. If a meal was available but I didn't feel hungry, I wouldn't eat it. If my body signaled that it wanted something "nutritious", I ate it. When I felt full, I stopped eating – even if I was leaving food on my plate.

When I arrived home, instead of my customary weight gain, my weight loss totaled an additional two pounds. That's how I knew that I finally "got" it.

Here's the reality: when you think something is wrong, it IS wrong, and it stays wrong and it brings you exactly what you don't want. When you stay in the energy of fat, you stay fat. When you stay in the energy of resistance, you get exactly what you don't want. When you think that whatever you put in your mouth is going to make you fat or keep you fat, it IS going to make you fat and keep you fat.

The truth is that Nothing Is Wrong with your body except that you think that something is wrong. You can love your body back into the weight and health that you want.

I now teach an extended course, along with personal coaching, called *"Loving Your Body Back into the Weight and Health You've Always Wanted"*. The basic ideas are very simple:

1. **Stop telling yourself that something is wrong with your body.** Stop talking about it, stop talking about how fattening food is, and stop discussing it with your friends and everyone else.

2. **Start checking in with your body to discover what it really wants to eat and examine your thoughts about what you are about to eat.** If you think that something is going to make you gain weight, then it will. So don't eat it. If you want to lose weight, then eat something that you think will make you lose weight. You will start to see shifts happen as you do this. It's quite remarkable, and it starts to become fun to play with it.

3. **Start putting yourself in the mindset of feeling good about your body.** Stop telling yourself that you hate your body or that you need to lose weight or that you want it to be different. Start actively and consciously loving your body (and download the free meditation below to help you do this).

It's so interesting to observe the results when you start to move into this energy. We've had many people come to Sedona for a Soul Adventures retreat, and although their stated reason for attending was something other than weight loss, once they were back in connection, weight loss seemed to follow naturally. One woman even posted a YouTube video about losing 17 pounds of what she called "protection weight" after she returned home from her Soul Adventure.

Stepping Stone #5 – *"Loving Your Body"* Meditation

We are now moving into the Clear Out phase of this book.

We've completed four processes related to Finding Out what's wrong and what's brought you to this place. We're now about to start Clearing Out this energy.

The first part of my spiritual process was more mental than anything else. It started out with therapy, lots of books, and readings with practitioners.

It wasn't until I started doing work that is designed to move energy and to connect my Self with the energy of the Divine that things really started to change for me.

Meditation is one of the core practices I do that keeps me centered and makes it easier for me to stay in the space of Nothing Is Wrong. I would guess that you already know the benefits of meditation, but suffice it to say that countless scientific studies have proven that regular meditation can improve your health, happiness and brain in all the following ways:

- Weight loss (which is why we're using it here!)
- Increased immune function
- Decreased pain
- Reduction in depression, anxiety and stress
- Increased social connection and emotional intelligence
- Improved ability to control your emotions and gain perspective
- Expanded sense of focus and attention
- Increased creativity, out-of-the-box thinking and improved memory

I am continually amazed to find out how many people meditate. I was at a business workshop recently in Los Angeles (not a spiritual workshop). The presenter (who is a meditator) asked the group how many of them meditate and had been doing so for more than five years. I was stunned that over one-half of the room raised their hands.

I was driving to Phoenix recently and listening to Alec Baldwin's Podcast *"Here's The Thing"* during which he was interviewing Jerry Seinfeld. Jerry said that he'd been practicing Transcendental Meditation since 1972! He credits it for a large amount of his success. Alec Baldwin agreed that maybe he needed meditation as a way to dissipate his persistent anger (Alec must be an 8!).

I'd like to gift you with a meditation that will actually bring you into the vibration of loving your body. Download the *"Loving Your Body"* meditation.

or go to http://thejourneytohappy.com/video7/

Do this meditation every day. It's only nine minutes, so it's easy to do it on a daily basis. It will help you drop the resistance that you have to your body. It works with any bodily condition because it's the resistance that creates all of the trouble. When we realize that and drop the resistance, things start flowing into their natural patterns.

Using the Stepping Stones on the Journey to Happy

Stepping Stone #1 – What's Your Story?

If this chapter has brought up more issues and thoughts about your body, then add them to your Awareness List, knowing that they are in the process of being healed.

Stepping Stone #2 – Change Your Story, Change Your Life

Do you realize how often people talk about their bodies, and food, and how fattening everything is, and how this is not healthy, and that's not healthy, and no matter what I do, I can't lose weight? **Stop talking about it!** You're simply reinforcing it and making it more and more difficult. Instead, talk about the things that you like or appreciate about your body – or say nothing at all.

Stepping Stone #3 – The Enneagram Fit

Here are some ways that the different Styles are prone to mistreat or neglect their bodies and how you can take good care of yourself.

- **Style One – The Perfectionist**

  Because they're so obsessed with perfectionism, Perfectionists are prone to engage in very excessive diets and cleanses – even anorexia and bulimia. They often use alcohol to self-medicate stress.

  Take care of yourself: Do things to release stress, such as giving yourself special treats just for the heck of it (for me, it's roses and massages). Meditate. Try yoga (and remember you don't have to do it perfectly).

- **Style Two – The Helper**

  Because Twos have such a craving for love, they often binge on food, especially sweets and carbs. This overeating is at odds with their desire to please their partner by looking good, and can result in bulimia. They are also prone to hypochondria as part of a dramatic need for connection with people around them.

  Take care of yourself: Spend less time doing things for others and more time for yourself, especially on things that you do alone. Be honest about what you want and don't "stuff it" with food.

- **Style Three – The Achiever**

  Because Achievers are constantly over-achieving, they work too much, and most of them don't take good care of their bodies. Conversely, because they care so much about how other people see them, if they exercise, they work out too much and to the point of exhaustion. They are also prone to excessive cosmetic surgery. They usually drink lots of coffee and sometimes consume other stimulants (like amphetamines) to keep themselves going.

  Take care of yourself: Stop working so hard. Schedule time in your calendar for exercise that feels good and that you truly enjoy (such as dancing, walking, hiking, etc.). Avoid exercise that feels difficult or punishing. It's most important for Threes to do something every single day for relaxation. Meditation is the best thing for Threes. Schedule vacations. When you go, leave everything at home and completely unplug.

- **Style Four – The Romantic Adventurer**

  Because Fours think that something is missing, they often overindulge with food or alcohol, trying to fill that hole. Many Fours typically don't enjoy physical activity.

<u>Take care of yourself</u>: It's important to pursue some type of exercise or movement that you enjoy. Eat only when you're really hungry and eat what you truly want to eat.

- **Style Five – The Investigator**

  Because Fives are usually so much in their heads, they tend to neglect their bodies and don't eat well. Often, they're sleep deprived. They can also be prone to drug abuse as an escape mechanism.

  <u>Take care of yourself</u>: Plan your meals for the following day. Know what you are going to eat. Schedule physical activity into your calendar and then do it.

- **Style Six – The Loyalist**

  Sixes are very rigid in their eating habits, sometimes to their detriment. Because Sixes are usually dealing with some kind of anxiety, they often abuse drugs and alcohol. They also overuse caffeine, which, ironically, can lead to more anxiety.

  <u>Take care of yourself</u>: Take advantage of your energy by engaging in vigorous physical exercise. Remember that there are no 100% right or wrong ways to do anything (like exercise or eating), so just do what feels good to you.

- **Style Seven – The Enthusiast**

  Ironically, because they are so positive, Sevens sometimes don't see the danger inherent in substance abuse. Of all of the Styles, Sevens are the most prone to addictions, and they will occasionally do dangerous things to their body to stay "up" including abusing drugs, especially painkillers. They are also among those most likely to indulge in excessive cosmetic surgery.

<u>Take care of yourself</u>: More than anyone, Sevens needs to develop healthful habits of eating, sleeping, and exercise that become a pattern they adhere to. Again, what's healthy for one person isn't necessarily healthy for another. Tune in to your body and do what makes you feel good.

- **Style Eight – The Aggressor**

Eights work too much and do too much. More than the other Styles, they tend to push themselves too hard and don't want to "waste" time on check-ups and self-care. Because they push themselves too hard and typically have high stress levels, they are highly prone to strokes and heart attacks.

<u>Take care of yourself</u>: Slow down, take hot baths, get a massage, and participate in physical activity that feels like fun (dancing, hiking) and doesn't feel like work.

- **Style Nine – The Peacemaker**

Because Nines are usually so full of repressed anger, they often eat too much or too little – the result of being disconnected from their bodies and their feelings. Their tendency to "space out" can lead to drug abuse (especially psycho-tropics) to alleviate their loneliness and anxiety. Some Nines don't like any physical activity; others over-indulge in exercise and push their bodies beyond what they can tolerate. Both extremes demonstrate the disconnection from the body.

<u>Take care of yourself</u>: Become consciously aware of your eating habits. Plan your meals for the next day so that you know what you will eat. Explore physical exercise that you like. Nines typically enjoy tai chi and other martial arts (especially the types that involve splitting boards!).

Stepping Stone #4 – Discover the Patterns

As discussed in the last chapter, I understand that my parents and I thought and felt the same way about our bodies. They weren't into healthy eating. My mother was constantly dieting. She didn't become thin until she became ill, and then she didn't want to eat at all. Ironically, after my mother died, my dad married a severely overweight woman. The two of them were constantly dieting. They would diet and lose weight and then gain it all back again.

As in the previous chapter, pull out your journal and list first how your parents thought about the following things and then how *you* think about them:

- Body Image
- Body Type
- Exercise
- Diet
- Supplements
- Traditional Medicine/Alternative Medicine

Observe the similarities and the areas in which you don't want to be similar. Just take that in.

I'm NOT saying that you look like a supermodel and you shouldn't want anything to be different with your body. What I AM saying is that after so many years of struggle, everything changed for me when I finally started to love my body. When I hated my body, I could go on every diet in the world and lose weight, but because I always thought and felt of myself as fat, the weight always came back. When I finally stopped talking and thinking about it all of the time and instead learned to check in with my body and listen to what it wanted, I went from a size 14 to a size 6, and I've stayed there for over five years.

Now I eat and drink whatever I want whenever I want it, and I've helped many, many people come into the space of loving their bodies with stunning results, including one woman in Massachusetts who has lost 90 pounds and kept it off for two years and another woman in California who is now a (healthy) size 2! This one shift is at the base of having a happy, healthy body.

What if I have a serious health issue such as cancer or heart disease or some sort of chronic illness?

Please understand that I'm not saying don't go to the doctor and stay home and try to feel good. What I am talking about here is you doing whatever is necessary to start shifting how you're feeling about it, how you're talking about it and what you're thinking about it.

There are many people who have had significant decreases in their symptoms by utilizing these principles. Norman Cousins who wrote the book *"Anatomy of an Illness"* was diagnosed with serious heart disease and a rare form of arthritis that was incredibly painful. He was told by his doctors that he realistically had only one year to live. As he documents in his book (which was also made into a movie starring Ed Asner), he went on a regimen of massive doses of Vitamin C and what he called a "prescription of positive attitude, love, faith, hope, and laughter" by watching Marx Brothers movies. In his book he said, "I made the joyous discovery that ten minutes of genuine belly laughter had an anesthetic effect and would give me at least two hours of pain-free sleep." He lived to be 75 years old – 36 years beyond his first dire diagnosis!

Louise Hay, who wrote *"You Can Heal Your Life"* and *"Heal Your Body"* was diagnosed in 1978 with cervical cancer which she was told was incurable and terminal. She is now 89 years old. She believes from her own experience that "all disease comes from a state of unforgiveness". In *"Heal Your Body"* she says, "I find that when we really love and accept and approve of ourselves exactly as we are, then everything in life works."

Use the *"Loving Your Body"* meditation. Come into the energy of truly loving your body and see what happens.

And if you enjoy that meditation, I have an entire series that is available on our web site.

or go to:
http://sedonasouladventures.com/meditations-jth/

Now let's deal with your money – the next hot button!

CHAPTER VI

NOTHING IS WRONG WITH YOUR FINANCIAL SITUATION
Bringing In Abundance

Have You Ever Asked Yourself, *"Why Is There Never Enough Money?"*

We're going to examine finances in two separate chapters – one about money and one about work. Although the two are closely linked, they're different. If you can release fear and worry about money, then it gives you more freedom to make decisions about the work you do and how you spend your time.

Almost Everybody (Rich and Poor) Thinks He or She Has a Money Problem

As a young child, I thought that our family had money. Even though that turned out to be untrue, I'm really glad my very formative years were spent thinking that we did.

My parents were solidly middle class. They both grew up on large farms in Iowa. In Iowa, land is money. That's so funny because I wrote those words today and then heard a radio report that farmland in Iowa is currently worth more than farmland anywhere else on the planet.

My parents both grew up in small, German Catholic communities. My grandmother Stangl had 20 children. My father was number nineteen! This was at a time when more children meant more farm hands, not more college tuition. My Grandfather Stangl had a tavern that he operated after Prohibition ended – so he had land plus a cash business. My mother's family had a farm, but they lost it during the Great Depression. The fall-out from this was intergenerational. Many years later, I found myself caught up in a pattern of belief that money can be suddenly taken away from you.

I think I thought that we had money because we had more than most of our friends. We always had a nice house and nice cars, we went to private (Catholic) school and wore uniforms, we were all going to college, we belonged to the country club, and we enjoyed dance, golf, and tennis lessons. My younger sister even had a horse. Even though things were tight sometimes, I thought that had more to do with the fact that there were six children in our family than anything else.

We moved to Ottumwa, Iowa when I was 12 years old. My father built a large nightclub, adding to the three bars that he owned with his two partners. Our house was in one of the nicest neighborhoods in town, right on the number five fairway of the golf course. We were members of the country club. We were considered the "elite of Ottumwa" (just saying that sounds so funny).

All hell broke loose when I was 13. I knew something was not okay with Dad (he was vomiting every morning) and things were tense between him and Mother. One summer morning, Mother went down to my dad's club and discovered a pile of unpaid bills. She came home and locked us out of the house while she talked to my dad. Nothing like this had ever happened before, and I was afraid.

After that, we had continual money trouble. Nothing was ever explained, which only added to the fear. But it was also very confusing because, although Mother always said that we didn't have enough money, there seemed to be enough for what my parents deemed important. They bought a larger, nicer home down the street, new cars, college tuition, etc. We kept up appearances and retained membership in the country club, had the dance, golf and tennis lessons, etc., but money was a continual issue after that. Mother even went to work, becoming surprisingly successful in sales.

When I got out into the world, I discovered that no matter what someone's background was, they could have major issues regarding money.

In law school, I was a law clerk in the Trust Department of a large bank in Omaha where I became acquainted with "trust fund babies" who thought they had money problems because they couldn't "live" on the vast sums that they would receive from their families' trust every month.

When I became a divorce attorney, almost all of my clients talked the same way about money. It didn't matter if they made $500 per month or $25,000 per month; it was never enough.

In my personal coaching work, it's the same thing. Clients who have millions in the bank talk just like my clients who are in debt. If money is an issue, there is the same continual fear.

If money is one of your issues, it can be difficult to let go of worry and come into the idea that Nothing Is Wrong. But, it's just like everything else. Money is energy. It is energy in constant circulation. The more we circulate out, the more we can allow it to circulate back to us.

When we worry about something, we bring it to us faster. When we worry about not having enough money, we remain in the energy of not having money, and money literally stays away from us.

The times that I have been most worried about money were the times when it didn't come. The more that I have let go of my worry about money, the more it flows.

The entire concept of Nothing Is Wrong is deeply tied with the concept of letting go. The more we can let go, the more astounding the results will be.

The Day $50,000 Dropped out of the Sky – You Might Not Believe This, But It Really Happened!

One of the most amazing experiences of my life was when I came to Sedona for the first time in January 1999. I had just started my 20th year of law practice, and I was completely burned out. I was working 60-70 hours per week and hated it so badly that I wanted to jump off of the nearest cliff. The worst part was that, even though I was generating large sums of money through my practice, my husband and I had incurred $50,000 in debt five years earlier (due to a strange set of circumstances) and I was never quite able to make any headway against it.

During those five years, I spent a lot of time praying and meditating, saying, "God, I'm so unhappy! Please tell me what to do!" Almost every time I did that I would hear a voice say, "Leave your law practice." I would immediately respond, "I can't do that! I've got a mortgage and two car payments! I'm the sole supporter, and I'm $50,000 in debt! I CAN'T leave my law practice!"

When I arrived in Sedona for the first time, I received the unmistakable message that I had to change my life (I'll tell you more about that in the next chapter). I had to leave my law practice, but how was I possibly going to do that? I came home and spent the next two weeks trying to figure this all out with my lawyer brain – an approach that, of course, never works.

Finally, I just threw up my hands. In my despair, I experienced a profound letting go. I said, "Okay, God, I get it that I have to do this, and I'm going to do it. So if it means selling the house and selling one car and living in the other one and never going anywhere again (I love to travel, so that would have been very difficult for me), okay, I'll do it. But you've got to give me some help here."

Less than eight hours later I got a phone call from one of my former clients. At the end of the conversation, he told me that he had just bought a new mortgage refinancing business. This was in 1999 at the start of the new "easy" mortgage lending trend that would ultimately be a factor in the meltdown of the real estate market in 2008. I asked him if it would be possible to re-finance my house to get a lower monthly payment.

He said he'd check and let me know. Ten minutes later he called back and said, "I can cut your mortgage payment in half, plus I can get you $50,000 in cash."

I had never told him that I was $50,000 in debt. Suddenly, in an instant, the weight of five years of worry was gone. It was gone within eight hours of asking God for help. It was gone within eight hours of throwing up my hands and surrendering.

Surrender Does Not Mean Giving Up

Surrender is one of the most beautiful words in our language when it is used in the manner which means *to let go*.

In Merriam-Webster, the first definition of surrender is "to cease resistance". The second is "to relinquish possession or control", and the final is "to agree to stop fighting, hiding, or resisting".

When we surrender – when we stop fighting, resisting, and trying to control everything, and instead, allow the wondrous energy of the Universe to work WITH us – magic can happen.

Surrender, in its deepest meaning, is the dropping of resistance. Whether we're talking about money or any other aspect of our lives, it is our resistance that is causing us trouble and causing our lack of peace and happiness.

So, when I surrendered, when I let go, suddenly $50,000 materialized, and the weight of owing that money was gone. I was unstuck. The excuse I had used for five years to keep myself stuck was suddenly gone. I had no more excuses.

Isn't it interesting that the two most amazing things that have happened for me – finally having the body that I wanted and leaving my law practice to create the business of my dreams – came when I was in the pit of despair and finally just threw up my hands in surrender? At the time, I didn't realize that I was practicing the concept of Nothing Is Wrong, but that's exactly what I was doing.

Stepping Stone #6 - The Gratitude Journal

One of the fastest and easiest ways to bring more abundance into your life is to be grateful for what you already have. Gratitude brings us into a higher energetic vibration. When we're feeling negative emotions – anger, frustration, jealousy – we are vibrating at a much lower frequency. What's worse is that we attract to ourselves exactly what we *don't* want and bring in more and more of it. Experiencing true gratitude is one of the easiest and fastest ways to bring yourself back into a higher and faster energetic vibration that will then attract everything that you DO want into your life.

We will be using this process for the next 30 days, as it takes 30 days to establish a new habit and a new vibration.

For the next 30 days, take three minutes (that's all!) each morning and write down five things for which you are truly grateful. It might be that you have a roof over your head, you have a car that runs, or that you have enough food to eat. Do you know how many people in the world can't say that?

The important part is that each thing that you write must be true, and you must believe it. If you run out of things, it's okay to repeat some of them if you have to, but it's really better not to. Just start writing about simple things that you are grateful for, like the sun rising every morning, which, of course, is not a simple thing, that's a huge thing, but it's one of the things that we so take for granted.

After you have written down your five for the day, take just a moment to close your eyes, breathe deeply, and truly FEEL the gratitude. The more you can infuse emotion into the process, the faster the energy will start to move. If you find you can't muster the feeling, it's okay. Just breathe and let it go. As you move more and more into the process, it will start to come. Don't force it.

Once you form the habit, you can utilize a Gratitude Journal to include other areas of your life. It's very powerful to use a Gratitude Journal for issues related to your body or your general sense of self. For example, write: "I appreciate that I have pretty brown eyes," "I appreciate that I am funny," or "I appreciate that I'm a good friend."

Using the Stepping Stones on the Journey to Happy

Stepping Stone #1 – What's Your Story?

Money is a hot-button for almost everyone. Are there more layers you want to add to your Awareness List? Add them now, being grateful that you're uncovering everything that needs to come up for healing.

Stepping Stone #2 – Change Your Story, Change Your Life

Stop talking about your money situation. Stop thinking about it obsessively. Stop commiserating with your friends. Talk about how wonderful it is that you have a job, you have a place to live, and you have food on your table.

Stepping Stone #3 – The Enneagram Fit

How does your Style think and feel about money and what can you do about it?

- **Style One – The Perfectionist**

  More than almost anyone, Ones don't ever believe that they have enough of anything – money, love, you name it. Order is the most important thing for them, so make sure that you have your affairs in order. Lighten up. Talk to a financial planner who can demonstrate to you that you are probably doing okay. If your affairs are not in order, you won't feel comfortable until you are at least taking steps in that direction.

- **Style Two – The Helper**

  Twos often have money problems because they're doing so much for everyone else that they don't keep enough for themselves. Stop excessive financial giving until you know that you are completely taken care of yourself. For a Two, that will feel selfish, but understand that taking care of your own needs is not the same as being selfish.

- **Style Three – The Achiever**

  Threes are very concerned with how they look in the world and will overspend to compensate for that. Healing for the Three has to do with authenticity. Don't spend to make people think better of you. Connect with your heart and take care of yourself by living by your standards.

More than almost anyone else, relaxing about money and knowing that Nothing Is Wrong is vitally important for this Style.

- ## Style Four – The Romantic Adventurer

  Fours often have money difficulties because they think that they are different. They are drawn to "creative" work, and they tell themselves the lie that one can't make money in a creative field. The key for them is to find their uniqueness (with no ego) and know that many, many people are drawn to things that are unique.

- ## Style Five – The Investigator

  Fives are smart, so very often they'll be financially solvent, but they are prone to live as cheaply as possible and to hoard money, which prevents its flow. Money usually isn't that important to Fives; they are more likely to view acquiring it as a game. Fully embracing abundance is the way to healing for the Five.

- ## Style Six – The Loyalist

  Sixes are typically very insecure about money and are constantly looking to be supported by others. They will stay loyal to people (and jobs, bosses, etc.) to maintain the false security that the job represents. Money seems like the answer to all problems for the Six. More than any of the other Styles, the Six must find a way to know that true security does not come from money; it comes from knowing that Nothing Is Wrong and that we are being taken care of in every moment.

- ## Style Seven – The Enthusiast

  Sevens are happy and enthusiastic and very often draw abundance to them because of that, but because of their enthusiastic natures, they can have the tendency to overspend. Financial discipline allows huge healing for the Seven regarding money.

- **Style Eight – The Aggressor**

  Eights believe that life is hard, so all parts of life are hard, including making money. They believe they must do everything on their own with no one to help them. Until that thinking is healed, they cannot make substantial amounts of money when working with other people is required. Eights do work very hard, so monetary compensation does usually result over a long period of time. Eights also believe that "if I want it, I should have it", so they have a tendency to overspend. Eights need to learn to relax about money issues and to fully incorporate the principle of Nothing Is Wrong. The more that they stop struggling, the more abundance comes (remember my story of the $50,000).

- **Style Nine – The Peacemaker**

  Because the Nine wants peace so badly, they settle. They settle for pretty much everything. Their way to true healing regarding money is to become very consciously aware of what they are doing in all areas of their finances – earning, budgeting, spending, saving, etc.

Stepping Stone #4 – Discover the Patterns

Look again at the list that you made and ask yourself, "How did my parents deal with money? What did they think about it? Did they save money? Do you save money? Did they never have enough? Do you ever have enough?" Look for the similar areas. Find what's not serving you and start doing something differently.

Stepping Stone #5 – "*Loving Your Body*" Meditation

Keep doing the "*Loving Your Body*" Meditation each day. Feeling good in your body has a positive effect on everything, including your financial situation.

Often, we find that clients who have severe money issues also have severe trust issues, namely not trusting that the Universe will provide. One woman who came for a retreat at Sedona Soul Adventures told us upon her arrival that she was unemployed with no savings and almost completely broke. She experienced her Soul Adventure, discovered what was causing her blocks, cleared them, moved back into connection, went home, and immediately landed her dream job! This sort of thing happens over and over again. It's so extraordinary. And it happens even more frequently when people start doing what they love instead of doing what they hate. We'll talk about that next.

I'm NOT saying that your money situation is perfect. What I AM saying is that when you experience gratitude for what you have and stay in the energy of excited expectation rather than constant dissatisfaction, that's when more money, more abundance, more flow, and more of everything comes to you.

So now let's talk about how you can bring that in through doing work that you love.

CHAPTER VII

NOTHING IS WRONG WITH YOUR WORK OR CAREER
Finding Your Life Purpose

Have You Ever Asked Yourself, *"What is My Life Purpose and How Do I Find It?"*

For most people, work and money go hand in hand. Most people work for money as opposed to doing what they love and allowing the money to follow.

We have many people who come to Sedona Soul Adventures who have been very successful in their careers, but they feel lost, empty, and dissatisfied. They haven't truly found their life's purpose. For many, they want work that is more meaningful, that truly feeds their souls, and that makes them feel that the work they're doing is important and makes an impact on the world.

How I Went from Being an Unhappy Divorce Attorney to Doing the Work of My Dreams

When I was growing up, I wanted to be a dancer and an actress. I practiced and performed, and I was pretty good. In college, I majored in theatre and dance and was frequently cast in high-profile roles that involved both acting and dancing. This was in the early '70s, and social revolution was in the air. My first husband, who was on his way to law school, felt that acting and dancing were frivolous and not socially relevant.

I wanted to pursue an acting career, but I had no financial or emotional support from my parents or husband. What's more, when I graduated from college, my husband had been accepted into a really good law school and it made sense for me to support him. So, I did what most people with a Bachelor's Degree in theatre and dance do. I became a secretary. I gave up my dream of being an actress and a dancer and became a really good typist and an excellent organizer.

Luckily, I had two wonderful secretarial jobs while my husband was in law school. First, I was the personal assistant to our Congressman from Iowa, Ed Mezvinsky, who was a member of the Judiciary Committee during Watergate. (Ed's son, Marc Mezvinsky, is now married to Chelsea Clinton.) Those years in Washington were fascinating times that fed my deep political interest.

After that, I became the personal assistant for Abe Fortas, the former Supreme Court Justice, who had left the bench and was in private practice. Fortas thought I was very smart and capable and would make a great lawyer. Spurred on in large part by his encouragement and his glowing letter of recommendation, I decided to apply to law school and was accepted.

Rather than staying in Washington, my husband got a great job in Omaha, Nebraska, so we moved back to the Midwest. Also, my mother's cancer had progressed and I wanted to be closer to her, so moving to Omaha made sense.

My husband was not encouraging of my plans for law school. Our 5 year marriage had always been shaky; I was only 19 when we married, and he was only 20. We separated and divorced shortly after I started law school.

During law school, I became very interested in alternative energy and solar energy as a way of leading us out of our dependence on fossil fuels (this was during the energy crisis of the 1970s). I wrote a Law Review article on the legal right to receive solar energy on one's land. (There is none – if you install a solar system on your home and your neighbor builds or grows something that shades it, in most states there's nothing you can do about it.) I wrote and lobbied for legislation in the state of Nebraska that would help alleviate that problem, and the legislation became law.

After graduation, I co-authored a book about solar energy with a group of architects and engineers from the University of Nebraska. I was traveling to speak at conferences all over the country. It was all a lot of fun, especially going places and presenting papers. I was speaking to large audiences (which appealed to the actress in me) and speaking about something that I felt was of real importance.

The work in alternative energy only took up about half of my time, and I wanted to do other work so that I could bring in additional income. I decided to start working with uncontested divorces. It was quick, easy, no muss, no fuss. Well, there usually was a little bit of muss and fuss, but that was to be expected.

Suddenly, it was all over. In 1982, in the middle of a huge economic crisis, President Reagan was elected, and funding was cut for the solar energy offices and solar tax credits. In six months, there was no work left for me in alternative environmental law. Before I knew it, I had to give up the second dream of my young life.

What did I do then? All I knew was that I didn't want to be a divorce attorney. However, people were calling me because I had done this work for four years and asking me to take their case. I didn't want to tell them no, so I decided instead to triple my hourly rate, thinking that people wouldn't want to hire me because I was too expensive.

Instead, higher prices seemed to fuel the growth of my practice. People must have thought, "If she's that expensive, she must be really good," and before I knew what had happened, I became what I now jokingly refer to as the Divorce Queen of Omaha, Nebraska.

I hated it. I loved the part that involved helping my clients, and I did a lot of work with abused children and women for which I'm very proud. I wrote and lobbied for the passage of the "Children's Trust Fund Act" which has generated huge amounts of funding for child abuse prevention programs in Nebraska.

But I hated fighting with other attorneys and fighting the system. I despised child custody cases because they were so destructive to everyone involved no matter the outcome.

I began my 20th year of law practice in January 1999. My mental and emotional state had become so bad that there were days when I wasn't able to get out of bed. I even had thoughts of suicide a few times because I felt so desperate and stuck, but I didn't have the guts to go through with it.

At this lowest-of-low points, I did an energy work session, and what came through was that I was supposed to do a retreat. I was trying to figure out where I should go when suddenly I thought, "Sedona." I didn't even know exactly where it was.

An old business contact had a friend with a small retreat house in Sedona. I contacted her and came to Sedona for what I thought would be just three days of quiet. When I arrived, Ranjita spent some time talking to me in front of the fireplace. After a short time, she said to me, "Your law practice is sucking the life force out of you."

I decided to do a session with her. It was one of the most extraordinary experiences of my life. I saw visions. What I identified as my High Self appeared to me as the Egyptian Goddess Isis, the winged Mother Goddess. She enfolded me lovingly in her wings, told me that she loved me, assured me that I was going to be okay, but then said that I must leave my law practice now. "If you don't, you're going to die like your mother did."

Though I had been told to leave my law practice in the past, this time the message finally stuck. I was the same age as my mother when she first became ill (46). I left Sedona knowing what I had to do.

I had to leave my law practice. I didn't know how in the world I was going to do it, especially considering that we were $50,000 in debt and I was our only means of support, as my husband Tom had just started a new business that was not yet producing income. I just knew that I had to do it, no matter what.

As I described in the last chapter about money, once I made that decision, once I became completely clear that this is what I was going to do come hell or high water, suddenly the $50,000 materialized (almost) out of nowhere.

I had emerged from the "lost" energy into the energy of "I'm leaving my law practice. I know what I'm going to do. I'm going to leave my law practice."

I set July 31, 1999 as my last day in practice, which gave me six months. I had 175 active cases. I took care of all of my clients and all of the cases. I helped the people who worked for me to get great jobs.

In Nebraska, it's considered a breach of confidentiality to sell a law practice, so I had nothing to sell except computers, office furniture, and books. Twenty years of work with nothing to show for it financially did not feel great, but leaving felt wonderful.

I told myself that I was going to leave for one year. I didn't see how I could go beyond that without income.

In May of that year, Tom and I decided to participate in a couples workshop with Ranjita in Sedona. We stayed at her place. When we went out hiking, she asked how my law practice was doing. I told her that as of July 31, I was leaving. She was amazed, saying that very often people say they're going to do something like that and then they never do. By the end of the weekend she said, "You know, once you've closed your practice, you should come out to Sedona for an entire month just to completely unwind from that energy." I told her that there was no way I could afford to do that.

But we kept talking and formulated a plan. I would help her with some legal and accounting work in exchange for staying at her place (and sleeping on the couch when she had retreat guests) for a very affordable amount. That September I stayed an entire month.

Looking back, that was one of the most important times of my life. I participated in a number of healing sessions with other practitioners whom I met through Ranjita. I knew that I was in the middle of an important healing process, transitioning from one life to another, and I knew I needed help.

Over the next three years, I repeatedly went to Sedona for a month or so at a time for deep healing work. I thought I would only be able to leave my practice for one year, but Tom's new Internet marketing business started taking off and he began supporting me both emotionally and financially, for which I am eternally grateful.

It was a delicious period for me. I thought that I was doing the work that I needed for my own personal growth—and I was! But, unbeknownst to me, I was also laying the groundwork for Sedona Soul Adventures. I was connecting with an amazing group of healers in a place known for its transformational healing energy.

After about a year of going to Sedona every few months (and staying for a month at a time), I would run into my new friends, and they would say, "When are you moving to Sedona?" I would always say, "I'm never moving to Sedona. I love my friends in Omaha. I love my house in Omaha. I'm never moving to Sedona." Well, never say never.

Suddenly, in 2001, three weeks before 9/11, I was in Sedona doing a session in the same room where my High Self had appeared almost three years before. My High Self came in again, and this time she said, "It's time to move to Sedona." I responded, "Why? What am I going to be doing in Sedona?" I got no response. One of the things I have learned over the years is that the High Self doesn't usually show you the complete picture, only the next step. Mine had shown me the next step.

My brain started working. I wanted to move to Sedona, but it made absolutely no sense from a financial standpoint. Tom had gone to work for his largest client and had a great job in Omaha (along with health insurance and stock options), and I had no idea what I was going to do in Sedona. But the one thing I had learned was how important it was for me to listen to what I was being told.

Within 24 hours of receiving that message, I got a phone call from one of my new Sedona friends who said, "I hear you're moving to Sedona. I'm leaving for India for six months to film a documentary. Would you like to rent my house?" It's a fabulous house, and the rent offer was almost too good to be true. I said yes.

I went back to Omaha. Tom was excited about moving to Sedona, so we put our house on the market. It sold in three days (the real estate agent had said that it would take six months) for more than what the real estate agent had predicted. I took that as a sign.

We moved to Sedona, and I sat there for six months awaiting some insights, but nothing transpired. I would pray to God and say, "I did what you told me to do. I came here. Now what?"

Suddenly, over those next few months, I started having dreams about what would become Sedona Soul Adventures. I knew and had worked with so many extraordinary healers in Sedona and, perhaps as importantly, I also knew which ones weren't that great. I saw how it was the private sessions and not group workshops that had made all the difference. I remembered how I had told certain friends who wanted to come to Sedona, "You should do a session with this person and this person and stay at this place and be sure to have dinner at Dahl & DiLuca." On a very small scale, I was already doing it. I had found my path. I realized then that my entire life had led me to this.

How Do I Find My Life Purpose?

I tell you all this to point out the simple truth that we are all living our life purpose right now. Nothing Is Wrong. You are fulfilling your destiny one step at a time. The key is to look for steps along the way, to listen to the information you're receiving, and to move in that direction.

I see now how everything that I have done in my life has led me to exactly where I am right now. It was necessary and important for me to go through the pain and unhappiness of my law practice. It was that pain and unhappiness and despair that led me to finally leave.

Some might say that I wasted 20 years practicing law, but that's certainly not the case. During that time, I learned a great many things. I learned that I loved helping people. I learned how to run a business. I learned how to read a balance sheet. I learned how to hire and fire people and how to listen to my gut when somebody looked good on paper but something still felt "off". I learned to listen to my intuition in dealing with a case and the different people involved. I learned that you can help some people, but you can only really help people who want to be helped.

I learned that I was a hard worker and dependable and that I would do what I told people I would do. I learned that I could let go.

Most importantly, I learned that real change and transformation are possible.

At each step of the way, I simply took the next step that was in front of me. Over the years, I've had many people say to me, "Oh, you must have been so brave leaving your law practice. That must have taken so much courage."

I never felt brave, I never felt like I was doing anything out of the ordinary. I was simply listening to what I was being told and then doing what I was being told. It took me five years to finally start listening, but once I started listening, each next step just seemed like the logical thing to do.

In my coaching practice, I work all of the time with people who want to leave the work that they're doing in order to do something else. Very often they don't know what it is. I've found that when you keep yourself locked in the energy of "I don't know what I'm supposed to do", then you stay in the energy of not knowing what to do. When you stay in the energy of "I hate my work", you stay locked in that energy and nothing can shift.

But, when you can bring yourself into a different energy, it's amazing what can happen. I see it all of the time when people come here to do a Sedona Soul Adventures retreat, and I see it all of the time in my coaching practice. I've helped people move from being a medical doctor into becoming an artist and having gallery showings. I helped one lawyer in Canada leave an unfulfilling corporate law practice and become an energy worker with a thriving practice.

I helped another lawyer discover that she actually loved her law practice; she simply wasn't doing it in a way that nurtured her. In the final session of her Soul Adventure, we talked about what would be perfect. She lives in Los Angeles and had just purchased a condo in Palm Springs, which is a two-hour drive. She said, "I would love to work four days per week and have each weekend to go to Palm Springs. I want to take only the cases I want – the ones I believe in – and I want to make the same amount of money." Before her Soul Adventure, she was telling herself that this would be completely impossible.

The more we talked, the more she could see how this could work. We designed what she was going to do, and when she went back to Los Angeles, her partners were more than happy to accommodate her. They were afraid that they were going to lose her completely. Instead, it was a win-win-win. She got what she wanted, her partners got what they wanted, and her clients got an attorney who really cared about their cases.

Of course, we don't just work with doctors and lawyers. People from all walks of life who do all different types of work come here to find and embrace their soul purpose and life mission. For some, it's changing into something else. For many people, it's finding the parts they love in what they're already doing and discovering how to get more of it.

Some of the most satisfying clients we work with are mothers who are stressed out and burned out. We clear out the blocks, bring them back into connection, and give them tools to not only maintain that connection but to continue to deepen it. They go home more committed to their families (and themselves) than ever before, but they do it in a way that is balanced and gives them joy.

Stepping Stone #7 - Tapping

Tapping comes in a number of different forms, and it has been around for many, many years. It is the very simple process of tapping with your fingers on different parts of your body. Different people will give you different explanations about why tapping works. I believe that it is related to the energetic meridians that flow through our bodies. This knowledge has been used for thousands of years in Chinese medicine. When you tap, stuck energy starts to move.

A psychologist who studied acupuncture popularized Tapping in the United States. He encouraged his patients to tap different acupuncture points with astounding results in alleviating fears and phobias. Tapping has now been used for a variety of different issues, and I find it generates an overall sense of well-being. If you would like to read all about it, there are thousands of websites and books on the subject. Suffice it to say it's easy and it works. I'm giving you the basic information you need to know so that you can start using this powerful tool in your life right now.

There is the long form of Tapping and the short form. We'll cover both here.

Tapping – Long Form

We're introducing this process for use with your work, but as with all of the processes, it can be used for any issue.

Read the directions all the way through before you start.

1. **Identify the precise issue.**

    What exactly about your work bugs you the most? Is it that you feel you aren't living your life purpose? Is it boring? Do you just simply hate it? Identify the precise issue. We will focus on one issue at a time.

2. Check in and rate your level of dissatisfaction.

Close your eyes and check in with yourself. Rate how you feel about this issue on a scale of 0-10, with zero representing no dissatisfaction or upset about your work or job and ten representing that you hate your work or your job, it's driving you crazy, or you're completely frustrated and you know you should be doing something else but you don't know what it is. Make a note of that number so you can compare it to how you feel when you complete the tapping.

3. You will tap in nine places (Illustrations are below).

For numbers two through nine, tap using two fingers of both hands.

1) The karate chop point (the fleshy part of your hand between the start of your wrist and the start of your pinky, as if you are doing a karate chop). For this point only, tap using all the fingers on either hand. It doesn't matter which hand you're tapping with or which hand you're tapping on.

2) Eyebrow – from the end of the eyebrow toward your nose.

3) Eyebrow – in the opposite direction away from the nose.

4) Under the eyes where you feel the bone.

5) Under the nose.

6) The chin where there is a crease.

7) At the collarbone (the knot at the end of the collar bone toward the center of your body – marked on the illustration as the "sore spot").

8) Heart chakra – on the breastbone in the middle of your chest.

9) Under your arm – where the bra would be if you wear a bra. Tap on just one side.

4. **As you tap in each place, say three times:**

    Using your precise issue, repeat it three times: e.g., "Even though I hate my work (or I'm frustrated that I don't know my life purpose/hate my boss, etc.), I deeply and profoundly love, accept, and respect myself just the way I am."

5. **As you say the words, focus on how badly this issue makes you feel.**

    This is a time to wallow in how "wrong" everything is so that the energy can be brought up and moved. Get into that emotion as much as you can.

6. **Complete the Tapping exercises in all of the places.**

    When you are complete, check in to see how you feel. On a scale of zero to ten, where are you now?

7. **Very often, as you are tapping, some other issue might come up.**

    For example, the thought, "If I leave my law practice, I will feel like I wasted 20 years of my life." If this occurs, do another round of tapping on that issue by saying, "Even though I will feel like I wasted 20 years of my life, I deeply and profoundly love, accept, and respect myself." As more and more issues come up, tap through each one. Give yourself the time that you need to tap through these issues as they come up. Do an entire round for each issue.

Tapping – Short Form

At least three times each day (when I wake up, once during the day, and before bed) I tap the karate chop point and say three times, "I deeply and profoundly love, accept, and respect myself just the way I am." It is incredibly powerful.

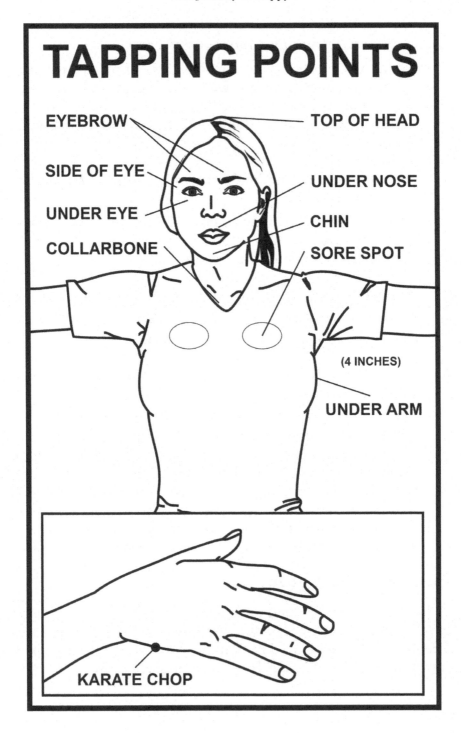

The objective of this process is to release you from the energy of "I hate my work" or "I don't know my life purpose" to move you back into the energy of excited expectation, but again, this will work on any issue.

Using Silent Meditation to Discover the Next Step in Your Life's Work

If you're in a position of knowing that you should be doing something else but you're not sure what it is, use silent meditation to discover the next step. Be silent, breathe deeply, and ask your High Self to show you the next step. Write down the answers in your journal. The answers might not make sense immediately, but as you continue on the path, they will make more and more sense.

Don't do what I did for five years. When I would meditate and ask questions about what I should be doing, I was always told to leave my law practice, but for five years I wouldn't listen. Because it seemed so impractical and impossible to my rational mind, I wouldn't even explore the possibility. I would stop the process before even giving it a chance to start.

Ask your question and listen to the answers. Be willing to take the next step. Sometimes the next step seems small and almost meaningless, but I can assure you that it isn't. Follow the path.

Sometimes the next step is a bigger step than we initially intended, but the results can be fantastic.

When we take the leap of faith, that's when the magic happens.

Right at the time that I understood that my next step was to move to Sedona, I happened upon the movie *"Indiana Jones and the Last Crusade"* while channel surfing. This is the one with Sean Connery playing Indiana's father.

At the end of the movie, the Nazis have shot Indie's dad in the stomach, and the only way Indie can save him is to solve a bunch of riddles and find the Holy Grail. Indie is told that he needs to take a leap of faith. He looks down and sees a chasm that is so deep that he can't even see the bottom of it. Taking the leap of faith means stepping into this chasm and what looks like certain death. He takes a deep breath and steps forward. Suddenly a path rises up to meet him, and he can cross the divide. When he felt the faith and believed and trusted, there it was. The path rose up to meet him.

He had to believe *Nothing Is Wrong, I'll be safe, I can take that next step.*

You can, too.

Using the Stepping Stones on the Journey to Happy

Stepping Stone #1 – What's Your Story?

Has reading this chapter brought up more issues or thoughts about your work? Add them to your Awareness List, knowing that you are on your path.

Stepping Stone #2 – Change Your Story – Change Your Life

Stop talking about how much you hate your work, your boss, your hours, your co-workers, how you're not making enough money, or whatever it is you're saying that's negative. Just stop talking about it.

Or, if you feel you're supposed to be doing something different but you don't know what it is, quit talking about how you don't know what it is. That keeps you stuck in the energy of "I don't know". If you have a strong desire, the Universe is telling you that you are moving in the right direction. Tell yourself, "I'm moving in the right direction. I'm on the path to finding out what it is that I'm supposed to be doing."

Stepping Stone #3 – The Enneagram Fit

It was perfect that I was an attorney for 20 years. The Eight loves to fight, and what a perfect venue – to get paid to fight with other people! But as I found myself moving toward my spiritual side, I wanted to use that energy to help people find the same kind of healing that I had found.

Look at your Style and see if this helps you:

- **Style One – The Perfectionist**

  Find work that will take advantage of your Perfectionist ways. The great thing about you is that you always get done what you say you will get done. If you're involved in work that you hate, look at whether or not it's because you believe other people aren't "doing it right". If you drop that judgment, will it help?

- **Style Two – The Helper**

  The Two is wonderful in the helping professions as long as they don't work too much. They can also be great at sales, as they have deep empathy for other people. Twos do too much and don't ask to be properly compensated. Then they get angry when people don't somehow "know" that they should be paying them more. Be clear about your expectations and say what you want.

- **Style Three – The Achiever**

  Threes are very hard working – that's one of the reasons they're called Achievers! They often find themselves in leadership positions. Because they're goal-oriented, Threes tend to choose work that truly satisfies their inner yearnings. It's very important for Threes to engage in work that is emotionally satisfying, so if you're not, put your high-achieving drive to work and create a situation that will totally fulfill you.

- **Style Four – The Romantic Adventurer**

  Fours are typically the most creative of the Styles, so you will often see them in the arts or teaching. If you are currently involved in work that you don't like simply to support yourself, either become happy with the work you're doing (appreciate what it does for you) or find a way to become open to the creative work that you do. "Do what you love and the money will follow" has become a truism because it happens to really be true.

- **Style Five – The Investigator**

  Because Fives are so intelligent, you will often find them in scientific or technical work. They're good at problem solving and analysis. If you're a Five and you're not doing work that satisfies that part of you, start moving in that direction.

- **Style Six – The Loyalist**

  Sixes are probably the most versatile in terms of doing work that will satisfy them. Because of their desire for security and their loyalty, you will often find them in large corporations or the military. They're hard workers and team players. If you're a Six and you don't like your job, then you're likely to become rebellious. If that's happening, find work where you feel like you can be part of a team.

- **Style Seven – The Enthusiast**

  Because Sevens are interested in so many different things, you will often find that they do more than one thing. Many entrepreneurs are Sevens because they're good at wearing many different hats. Sevens are good in emergencies and good at solving problems because they can see things from so many different perspectives. If you are a Seven and working as an accountant or doing work that is the same thing over and over, start to explore something that will give you more range.

- **Style Eight – The Aggressor**

  Eights work too hard and they think that they have to do everything by themselves. Stop working so hard and figure out ways to delegate (as an Eight, this is something I constantly have to keep figuring out). Eights excel in areas where they can take charge.

- **Style Nine – The Peacemaker**

  Nines are excellent listeners, so they're wonderful mediators and adept at work that brings people together. If you don't like your work, you are probably spending too much time focused on things that don't matter. Find someone to help you stay accountable to working only on what is significant.

Stepping Stone #4 – Discover the Patterns

Both of my parents worked too hard. They believed that hard work would always get you what you want. My father was self-employed, and when my mother was forced to go to work, she became very successful in sales and was self-employed. Of their six children, four of us are self-employed.

I am wired to work too hard, and all of my siblings also work too hard. I am constantly reminding myself to "work smarter, not harder". I know that more comes when I don't push, but I am constantly holding back the German farmer mentality that I was raised with and reminding myself to practice what I preach.

How did your parents "do" work? Did they hate their work? Did they love it? Was it emotionally and financially satisfying? What are the similarities between what they did and what you are doing regarding work, and what does that say to you? What is one thing that you can do differently?

Stepping Stone #5 – *"Loving Your Body"* Meditation

Keep doing the *"Loving Your Body"* Meditation each day. Feeling good in your body has a positive effect on everything, especially the work you are doing each day.

Stepping Stone #6 – Gratitude Journal

If this is an issue for you, use your Gratitude Journal to start moving the energy. Every morning as you write in your Gratitude Journal, write something positive about the work you're doing now. For example, as much as I disliked practicing law, there were a number of things that were good about it – I liked helping people, it was financially lucrative, and it made me feel like I was part of something larger than myself.

Express gratitude that you are in the process of finding your Life Purpose. You can write, "I know that I'm in the process of finding my Life Purpose," or "I'm grateful that I'm on the right path." You will be amazed at how this simple statement can change things around very quickly.

I'm **NOT saying** that your job or work situation is perfect and that you shouldn't want to change things. What I AM saying is that staying in the energy of "I hate my work" or "I don't know what I should be doing" will keep you stuck. Stay in the energy of excited expectation, knowing that you are living your life purpose and see how the magic starts to unfold.

Next comes one of the most challenging areas – your relationships.

CHAPTER VIII

NOTHING IS WRONG WITH YOUR RELATIONSHIPS

Taking the Other Person Off the Hook

Have You Ever Asked Yourself, *"Why Am I Not Being Loved in the Way That I Want To Be Loved?"*

Our Deepest Desire – For Someone to "Get" Us

Although many people believe that our deepest desire is to love and be loved, I believe that it goes even deeper than that. We can feel love *for* people, and we can feel love *from* other people like our spouses, parents, children, friends, etc. But there is nothing more delicious than to connect with someone who really "gets" you – who knows everything there is to know about you – your good points and your not-so-great points, your secrets and quirks – and still thinks that you're great. That is truly the definition of unconditional love.

Unconditional love – how over-used has that phrase become? I hear so many people say that they want it, and so many books have been written about it, but have you ever actually experienced it or truly given it (except possibly with a baby?) Probably not, because it's so difficult! Your husband drives you crazy, your wife doesn't understand you, your kids are lazy/ sullen/disrespectful / rebellious / lacking ambition/difficult, your siblings and parents are too demanding, and your friends are not really there for you. These are the things that I hear from people most of the time.

The people in our lives don't understand us. They don't understand how hard we're working. They don't appreciate all that we do. They don't forgive us our trespasses. They don't try to help us. Instead, they are usually giving us a hard time.

Husbands won't pick up after themselves, won't help with childcare, and want to spend the weekend watching sports rather than helping their wives and connecting with them, even though the wife has had a tough week, too.

Wives are insisting that husbands do, do, do all weekend long rather than allowing them to have even a nanosecond of relaxation after the long, difficult week that they experienced.

...and neither one is usually getting the type, style, or frequency of sex that they want.

Children are expected to do well in school, do what they're told, excel in sports, and participate in other activities.

"If you would only be..." or "If you would only do..." are phrases that are constantly used in relationships.

"If only my husband would help me, my life would be better."

"If only my wife would let me do some of the things that I want to do, my life would be better."

"If only my kids would (fill in the blank), my life would be better."

Well, let me be very bold:

It's Never about the Other Person Doing Something to You (or Not Doing Something); It's Always about Your Own Healing

The Universe brings people into our lives to assist in our own healing and evolution. Every single person who is in my life in even a small way has had an impact of some kind.

The concept of Nothing Is Wrong is all about taking personal responsibility for your life. You brought people into your life energetically to heal your issues. If you've brought in an angry person, where is the unhealed anger in you? If you've brought in a lazy person, where is the laziness in you and why does it bother you so much? If you've brought in a dishonest person, where are you not being honest with yourself?

Stop blaming others and discover what it is that *you* are meant to learn.

When someone says something to us that hurts us, usually the only reason that it triggers an emotional response is because we're afraid that what he or she is saying is true. Think about it. If you're afraid you're a bitch, and you don't want to be a bitch, and someone calls you a bitch, the only reason that it hurts is because you're afraid that you're a bitch. If someone calls you a book, that wouldn't have any effect on you, because not only is it not true, it simply doesn't make any sense. You wouldn't be angry; you would just be mystified.

The reason husbands and wives (or boyfriends/girlfriends/ partners) can hurt each other so quickly and deeply is because they know just what to say and do to make it hurt the most. When you know on a deep level that Nothing Is Wrong with you, those kinds of words can't touch you. When you know that Nothing Is Wrong with the other person, you stop saying those kinds of hurtful things to them, and you treat them in the way that you wish to be treated.

One of the most impactful books that I have ever read is *Radical Forgiveness* by Colin Tipping. The premise of this book is that before we're born, we make soul agreements with each other designed to aid in our soul's healing and progression. Our souls get together and have this cosmic meeting – think of it as a big conference room in the sky.

In this pre-lifetime conference, soul agreements are made – "Okay, last time you killed me, so this time I'll kill you," or "Last time you killed me, but this time I'll do something to break the cycle (such as forgiveness) so we're off of this particular karmic wheel."

Just imagine for a moment that it's true, then think about your relationships. What if the person who did something terrible to you was only doing it because of an agreement that you both made prior to coming into this lifetime? It's an arrangement that you (that Highest part of you) not only agreed to, but also considered to be in your best interest for the highest evolution of your soul.

Wow! That turns everything on its head.

Suddenly, the people who are "doing" things to you are actually giving you a huge gift – the gift of awareness and higher consciousness.

Even better, once you see it this way, you can stop it. "Okay, I got the lesson, I don't need any more of that."

Create the Relationship of Your Dreams by Taking the Other Person Off the Hook

The problem with blaming other people or holding them accountable for your happiness is that it gives them control over your life and happiness. It makes you the victim. When you take full responsibility for everything in your life, it's liberating and empowering. By realizing that Nothing Is Wrong with you and Nothing Is Wrong with them, it adds up to Nothing Is Wrong with the relationship. It doesn't mean that you don't want more and better; it just means that you can come from the energy of love and excited expectation – a much more delightful – even blissful – place from which to come.

How I Went from Co-dependent, Dysfunctional Relationships to Loving Myself

I was brought up in the '50s and '60s. I was taught that a woman's primary objective was to "catch" a husband. From that perspective, I did a great a job – I caught three!

I was very focused on boys and had my first boyfriend at age 12. From then on, I had a boyfriend or husband almost continuously.

When I was 13, my father fell in love with another woman (although I didn't know it at the time) and started abusing alcohol. My mother had to save the day for us financially. The model for me (at this very impressionable age) was an unavailable man, the woman as the provider, and the idea that even happy marriages don't last. I'm not blaming my parents; I'm saying that this was the unconscious message that I took in.

When I saw the emotional and financial devastation that happened to my mother as a result of my father's drinking, I think I (unconsciously) vowed to never put myself in that position. At the time I entered college (1970), the women's liberation movement was just starting to happen, so the idea of women supporting themselves and not being dependent on men made perfect sense to me.

Looking back, I see how my life mirrored my mother's. Her life patterns were showing up in my life patterns. I chose men who were unavailable and whom I needed to support financially. The choices weren't conscious, of course ("I'm looking for someone who's unavailable and I'll have to take care of! That sounds like a great idea!"), but the pattern was unmistakably there.

My first serious boyfriend was attending college in another city. My first husband was a law student, studying all of the time and never home. I worked to put him through law school, and as soon as he got a great job, I left. I was then in a relationship for seven years with someone who was so emotionally distant that one month after my mother died, he announced that it was time for me to "get over" her death, I had had enough time grieving, and I needed to stop crying about it.

After that, I prayed to God to bring me a "nice guy". A few months later, while traveling in Holland with my sister, I met the man who would become my second husband – another long distance relationship. After he had moved to the US and we got married, I put him through college. I always thought that I would have children, but when he refused to accept a fantastic and lucrative job offer, I realized that if I had a child, I would have two children to support – the child and my husband.

After I left my second husband, I started a relationship with an American who was living in Tokyo. Talk about unavailable – he was halfway around the world! The end of that relationship marked the beginning of really looking at myself and what I was doing with my life and taking responsibility for what I had created.

Following a disastrous trip to Tokyo, my law partner intervened (God bless you, Ken!) and I went through out-patient co-dependency treatment, a 12-step program that showed me how co-dependent I had become not only in my love relationships but also in my relationships with my family and clients in my law practice. I started to understand how children who grow up in homes with alcoholism or other abuse think that the insanity that comes with it is "normal". With my therapist, I pursued the practice of discovering the life patterns that I was mirroring from my parents (which we discussed in Chapter 4). I broke up with the guy in Tokyo and started digging deep.

As part of my codependency treatment, I made the commitment to stay out of romantic relationships for one year so that I could focus completely on my healing.

The spiritual part of my life became my biggest focus. I discovered breathwork and started doing it on a regular basis with a practitioner in Omaha. I started having experiences that were absolutely ecstatic, connecting with the Divine in very deep ways.

I took full responsibility for everything I had created in my life. After one year of no relationships, I decided I wanted to create a relationship that was in harmony with the spiritual principles that I was trying to live. I attended a relationship workshop and wrote out a list of everything I wanted to manifest. I met Tom 2 weeks later. When I met him, he was on a spiritual path, he felt very emotionally available, and he even lived in the same town! He had all but two of the things that were on my list.

What I didn't realize – until it was too late – was that we were both still focused on what was wrong.

When I first met Tom, he was a practitioner I went to for help – to "fix" me because I wasn't okay. My therapist knew Tom and advised against entering a relationship with him because (she said) this imbalance would always be there, plus there was the financial imbalance. My ego didn't want to hear that, so rather than stop seeing Tom, I stopped seeing my therapist. And, of course, she was right. That relationship never changed. I was trying to be a spiritual person, a "better" person, but I STILL felt and believed that there was something genuinely wrong with me that needed to be changed.

At the same time, I wanted to be loved and adored. I wanted someone who loved all of me, including my anger.

But, I didn't love those parts of me, so how could Tom?

Both of us were so focused on what was wrong with me that it became a vicious cycle. And of course, my reaction to the scrutiny was to focus on what (I thought) was wrong with him.

Looking back, it's so curious that even though I talked about leaving many times, ultimately, this time I wasn't the one who left. I had decided about one year earlier that I was going to stick it out. We had the business, the house, the dog. We had a lot in common on many levels. I kept telling myself that if we were truly spiritual people, we "should" have been able to make it work. No one in any of my previous long-term relationships had ever left me. I was always the one to go.

But this time I needed the jolt. He not only left, but he did it very abruptly and with absolutely no warning. We were having a usual kind of argument when he jumped out of his chair, and ten days later he was in Bali. Our 20-year marriage was over.

It was painful, but I'm so glad he did it that way. I needed to come face to face with my deepest fear – the one that said, "Oh my God, maybe there really IS something wrong with me. Someone left me for the first time in my life."

What astonishing healing can come from having the rug pulled out from under us! First, we're stunned; the wind has been knocked out of us. Then, we're on the ground asking, "What the heck was that?" Finally, we have to pull ourselves up and figure out, "What just happened?" "Why did I create that?" "What's the lesson?" and "What do I need to do?"

During that time, I did many, many sessions with the amazing practitioners here at Sedona Soul Adventures. I delved into the shadow aspects of my personality and began to love and embrace them, rather than push them away. Though I had done a tremendous amount of work in the years leading up to this experience, I realized that there were still some remaining pieces of myself that I didn't love. This was my chance to change that.

I saw how I had used my anger as a weapon and as a defense, but I also started to understand for the first time that my anger was a huge part of my life force, my drive, my zest for life, and my enthusiasm. It is a gift, not a curse. It is to be celebrated and modulated, not pushed away.

Paradoxically, when that energy moved, my anger started to dissipate – not only with Tom, but also with everyone and everything.

Tom came back from Bali for a few weeks to pack up and move out and move to Bali permanently. I was a mediator for 15 years during my divorce lawyer practice, and I knew exactly what he would want. We settled everything in two hours.

He has been a huge blessing in my life, and I appreciate the entire experience so much now that I've been able to Find Out, Clear Out, and Bliss Out. I was able to Find Out – really see what was happening and how I had created this for my own healing. I was able to Clear Out – get rid of the pieces of self-judgment that I was still carrying. And, I was able to Bliss out – no longer staying in the energy that something was wrong. Instead, I discovered the joy of truly loving myself.

Another interesting result is how this has been reflected in Sedona Soul Adventures. When Tom and I were together, we had some couples who came for retreats, but not a lot. Now that I am clear on this, over the past five years we have had so many couples whose relationships have been transformed by doing a Couples Retreat. It's mind boggling! And I'm so proud of the fact that last year, GuideDoc named Sedona Soul Adventures the #1 Couples Retreat in the US!

The couples who come to us are usually in some kind of crisis. While the details are always different, the cause is almost always the same: they think that something is wrong with the other person, and they want them fixed. When we help them Find Out and Clear Out their own unhealed parts, the two of them can finally Bliss Out as a couple.

We recently had two people here from California who had been married for over 12 years and have two adorable children. They started the marriage really loving each other, but they had grown apart, the sizzle was gone, and each was focused completely on what was wrong with the other. They experienced individual sessions to work on their own healing and then came together to participate in joint sessions that brought them into a deep connection. After they had returned home from Sedona, the husband wrote to say that when they were on their way to Sedona, he thought that when he returned he'd be filing for divorce (he had already contacted a lawyer). Instead, through their Soul Adventures retreat, the marriage was re-born and renewed.

It's so ironic that after 20 years of doing divorces for people, I'm now helping more and more people stay together and stay together in a wonderful, fabulous way.

What if I'm in a relationship where there IS something serious happening – my partner is physically or emotionally abusive, abuses alcohol or drugs, or is cheating on me?

During the 20 years that I was a divorce attorney, I saw many marriages end because of infidelity, physical and emotional abuse, or alcohol and drug abuse. I also spent many years representing children in Juvenile Court where abuse had taken place. These are certainly situations where it feels like something is very wrong, and I have seen many families torn apart in these circumstances. It's heartbreaking.

Drug and alcohol abuse and physical and emotional abuse have deep psychological and emotional underpinnings. As I discussed earlier in the book, the concept of Nothing Is Wrong does not mean that we condone behavior that is illegal or immoral or pathological.

Drug and alcohol abuse and physical and emotional abuse require the intervention of competent professionals, especially in the area of withdrawal from drugs and alcohol, as there are serious physical effects on the body.

At Sedona Soul Adventures we do not allow people to participate in our retreats if they are abusing drugs or alcohol because we are not a medical facility and do not have the necessary expertise that is required. However, we have had many people over the years who have come to us to deal with the emotional and spiritual aspects of their treatment after they have completed a rehabilitation program. It's been so gratifying.

We have also had many people come to us who are in a relationship with someone where abuse is an issue. Because each retreat is customized, we get to the root of the situation with each person.

What do they want? Do they want to stay? Do they want to go? What is the lesson for them? Can healing happen in such a way that the abuse stops? Can they come into compassion with their partner even if they decide that they must leave the relationship? Every situation is different, but each person has the ability to find their own truth and their own strength for their particular experience and outcome.

The issue of infidelity is one that we deal with very often in our couples retreats. The first question is always what do each of you want? Do you want to stay together or do you want to end the relationship? And, of course, Nothing Is Wrong with either decision.

Both of those choices have huge difficulties and major consequences. For some people, they find that they simply can't stay in a situation where they feel that they could never trust the other person again. For others, the thought of ending everything is too overwhelming. The marriage is over, the family is torn apart, the emotional and financial consequences are devastating – it's almost too much to even think about.

In light of all of this potential devastation, many people try to do everything that they can to put the marriage back together and come back into a place of trust and connection, and that's what's so wonderful about the work we do here.

When you can talk about it and when you can let everything out into the open, you can heal. It's difficult, it's hard – but the healing can happen. We've seen it over and over again. There's the healing that has to happen for each person individually and then there's the coming together and the rebuilding of trust and learning how to communicate with each other on a heart level again – or maybe even for the first time. It's miraculous when two people can come back into a place of love and trust with each other after so much heartache and pain.

I must say that after 14 years and thousands of people, it still amazes me what can happen here. People come to us on the brink of divorce and then turn it around.

We had a couple who came to us recently because the husband had been unfaithful. When they first arrived, they both told us that they didn't think that there was any hope. The wife didn't think that she could ever trust him again. Through her own individual sessions, she was able to come into a level of forgiveness with him and was even able to come into compassion with him for the insecurities that he suffered that had led to this. He was able to see that his wife really loves and appreciates him even though he hadn't felt that way before the affair. Another couple who came last year and rebuilt their relationship after an infidelity by the wife was able to weather the storm. They even came back again this year to celebrate and reinvigorate their healing and, as they said, "take our love to the next level."

If this issue has been haunting you, I first want to say that I'm so sorry. I'm so sorry for your pain and hurt and anguish. But I also want to tell you that there's hope. I know it. I've seen it. I've seen the healing take place and people come out the other end. We're all human. We all make mistakes, and sometimes the mistakes are more vicious and horrendous than we think we can bear, but you can bear it. You can make it through it.

If your partner has cheated, you're at a crossroads. You need to decide what you are going to do. I urge you to get help with this. This is one of the most critical times in your life, and the decisions that you make now will be affecting you (and your family) for the rest of your life. What do you truly want? What do you need? Now is the time to really be looking for your own healing as well as the healing of the relationship.

Certainly, a retreat (where you immerse yourself in your healing) is the best choice. What makes our retreats so unique and special is that they are customized for each couple and the sessions are all private sessions, not in groups. We spend a lot of time talking to each of you separately before you come to Sedona to uncover all of the issues that need to be healed. We then custom design the retreat for exactly what the two of you need. During your retreat, you'll work in private one-on-one (or two-on-one) sessions. We have over 40 practitioners, many of whom have over 20 years of experience working with couples.

The privacy of the sessions is so key. Many people don't feel comfortable in a group setting, and they don't want to talk about their most private issues in front of a bunch of strangers. There is also a strange dynamic that can sometimes happen in group settings where the group seems to "take the side" of one person, identifying one as the "good guy" and the other as the "bad guy", and the other person can feel ganged up on. That doesn't help the healing! The privacy of the one-on-one sessions and the skills of the practitioners truly create a space where both parties feel safe.

Stepping Stone #8 – Restore Your Relationship and Rewire Your Brain with Affirmations

Although Affirmations have been around for many, many years and are often considered a basic type of process, I have saved them for the end for a simple reason. Affirmations can be tremendously powerful when used properly – and the key is to use them properly.

Over the past few years, I've become fascinated with recent books that discuss the fact that we can actually change our brain chemistry. Up until the last decade or so, scientists thought that the makeup and functionality of our brains were fairly static. Now, they're finding that our brains have a surprising amount of plasticity.

Perhaps what's even more amazing is that we've discovered that the brain can be changed with something as simple as using Affirmations.

Affirmations can be written, spoken, or thought. They are positive messages that are used repetitively to alter the way we think (and therefore feel) about something. Examples of Affirmations are:

- "I am a beloved child of God."
- "I have everything I need to be completely happy and successful."
- "I love and adore my husband, he loves and adores me, and we are gloriously happy."

When we recite Affirmations, hormones are released that rewire our brains. It's exercising for your brain much like you would exercise your body! Affirmations trigger the release of feel-good hormones that actually cause the brain to form clusters of positive thought neurons.

Affirmations, therefore, operate as a kind of pattern interrupt. They can reverse negative thinking and negative emotions.

Here are three critical things to keep in mind as you practice Affirmations:

1. **Affirmations must be positive statements.**

   Write "I love my husband" as opposed to "We aren't going to have any more fights." The Universe doesn't hear a negative. When hearing, "We aren't going to have any more fights," the Universe receives, "Fights. Okay, send them more fights!"

2. **Make it a personal statement.**

   Use "I" when referring to yourself or "we" when referring to a couple so that the Universe knows that you're not talking about someone else.

3. **Write Affirmations in the present tense.**

   Many people make the mistake of writing Affirmations in the future tense, e.g., "We will have a more loving relationship." Instead, write "We have a loving relationship" as if it were already exactly as you want it.

In addition to that, keep the following critical steps in mind:

   a) Feel good while you're doing it. If it doesn't feel good, stop doing it.

   b) Make it as specific as possible without feeling like you are making it up.

   c) You need to believe that there is at least a kernel of truth in what you're saying.

Affirmations work because you're establishing a direct connection with the energy of the Universe. However, if you don't actually believe what you're writing or saying, you can do more harm than good because you're increasing the energy of what you don't want.

For example, if you feel like you hate your spouse, your relationship is horrible, and you feel unloved and misunderstood, the moment you write an affirmation such as "I love and adore my husband, he loves and adores me, and we are gloriously happy," your subconscious mind will rebel against the lie and you'll begin to think, "We're NOT gloriously happy, we're completely miserable, and I wish he would just drop off the face of the Earth!" These thoughts perpetuate feelings of anger, frustration, bitterness, and hopelessness.

Instead, use an Affirmation that is leading to where you want to be. For example, "There is a part of me that loves my husband. There is a part of my husband that loves me. We are connecting with the love that we have for each other."

Find a statement that has at least a kernel of truth in it and make it as specific as you can without being false. If you start to feel bad while you're writing it, that emotion is telling you that this is not the correct Affirmation. Keep trying until you find one that feels true and real and specific and hopeful.

Entering the vibration of love through your Affirmations can bring you to knowing and understanding that Nothing Is Wrong with your relationship. You loved this person once. Returning to that vibration is easier than you may think.

Using the Stepping Stones on the Journey to Happy

Stepping Stone #1 – What's Your Story

This chapter might have brought up more issues for you around your relationship. If so, add these to your Awareness List. We want everything out in the open!

Stepping Stone #2 – Change Your Story, Change Your Life

Stop talking about all of the terrible things concerning your partner (or your friends, your co-workers, your mother, or anyone else with whom you are experiencing relationship problems). If you want to talk about it, go to a competent couple's therapist or come and do a Soul Adventure for couples. We'll talk about it, but we'll be talking about it in a constructive and meaningful way. Stop allowing other people to trash their partners in front of you. It simply adds to the negative energy.

Stepping Stone #3 – The Enneagram Fit

Knowing how your Style fits with your partner's Style is invaluable. It's not a coincidence that I was an Eight married to a Nine. Eights want to fight, and Nines want peace at any price! What a loaded combination! But it's so perfect. Eights need to heal their anger and respect boundaries, and Nines need to feel their anger and set boundaries. It's the perfect match for healing the unhealed parts.

The following will show you to Stop This and Do This if you want the relationship of your dreams:

- **Style One – The Perfectionist**

  Stop This: being critical and nitpicky.

  Do This: be the loyal, helpful person that you are naturally wired to be.

- **Style Two – The Helper**

  Stop This: being needy, expecting the other person to read your mind, being possessive, and giving with a hook – if you truly want to do something for the other person, do it with no strings attached.

  Do This: be the generous, warm, and nurturing person that you are wired to be. Twos are the best at making their partners feel really loved.

- **Style Three – The Achiever**

  Stop This: being dishonest (there are no such things as little white lies, there are only lies), focusing so much on your work to the exclusion of your relationship, and being impatient.

  Do This: accept and value your partner and be playful and giving.

- **Style Four – The Romantic Adventurer**

  Stop This: jealousy, self-absorption, the "nobody understands me" attitude.

  Do This: continue being the empathetic, gentle, romantic, and passionate person that you are wired to be.

- **Style Five – The Investigator**

  Stop This: being negative, suspicious, and withdrawn.

  Do This: continue being the kind, perceptive, and trustworthy person that you are wired to be.

- **Style Six – The Loyalist**

  Stop This: being sarcastic, controlling, suspicious, and inflexible.

  Do This: continue being the loyal, supportive, reliable, and fair person that you are wired to be.

- **Style Seven – The Enthusiast**

  Stop This: being distracted, narcissistic, and possessive.

  Do This: continue being the fun-loving, adventurous, generous, and caring person that you are wired to be.

- **Style Eight – The Aggressor**

  Stop This: fighting (!!!), being demanding, and nit picking.

  Do This: let your sweetness and vulnerability come out and continue being the caring and committed person that you are wired to be.

- **Style Nine – The Peacemaker**

  Stop This: being passive-aggressive, stubborn, and defensive.

  Do This: continue being the gentle, supportive, and loyal person that you are wired to be.

Stepping Stone #4 – Discover the Patterns

How was your parents' relationship? Were they happy? Was there abuse or dysfunction? Did they focus on what was good or bad? Who ran the show? Who runs the show in your household? Were they committed to their relationship or just going through the motions? How are you repeating their patterns and how can you change the ones that are no longer serving you?

Stepping Stone #5 – *"Loving Your Body"* Meditation

Continue doing the *"Loving Your Body"* Meditation each day. Feeling good in your body makes you want to have more sex – a win-win for both of you!

Stepping Stone #6 – Gratitude Journal

If your relationship is an issue, add gratitude for your partner into your Gratitude Journal, such as:

1. I love his/her beautiful blue eyes.
2. I love that he/she likes dogs.
3. I love that he/she is good at his/her job.
4. I love that he/she has things that he/she enjoys, like painting or tennis, etc.
5. I love that he/she loves our children.

I once coached a woman who was ready to leave her husband. One of her biggest complaints was that she had a demanding job, and he wouldn't help her with the children or the house. During our first coaching session, I had her start a Gratitude Journal about the things about him that she actually liked. Within 48 hours, he started doing the dishes. She didn't even ask or nag; he just started doing it!

Stepping Stone #7 – Tap Out Your Frustrations

Use both the short form and the long form. When you're feeling particularly disenchanted, tap through each spot saying, "Even though I dislike my wife/husband right now, I deeply and profoundly love, accept, and respect myself just the way I am."

Using the short form (tapping the karate chop point and saying, "I deeply and profoundly love, accept, and respect myself just the way I am.") can have a profound effect especially if you feel an imbalance in the relationship (you give too much, or you feel the other person doesn't love you as much as you love them).

I'm NOT saying that your partner is perfect or that you should stay in an unhappy marriage (I didn't), and I'm certainly not saying that you should stay in an abusive relationship. What I AM saying is that people flourish when they are surrounded by the energy of love. When they feel love, they are much more likely to give love and appreciation back. Think back about the things that first brought you together. There were things that you loved, and you overlooked the things that you didn't love. We're all human. We all have our faults. Our deepest desire is to love and be loved and to be accepted for who we are. What a gift to be able to give and to receive!

And now that we've seen that Nothing Is Wrong in the particular areas of your life, let's see how Nothing Is Wrong with the World.

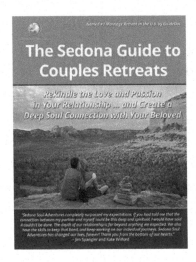

To download a free copy of our *"Sedona Guide to Couples Retreats"*

or go to:
http://sedonasouladventures.com/
couples-retreat-guide/jth/

Watch a video of me talking about our Couples Retreats.

or go to:
http://sedonasouladventures.com/retreats/couples-retreats/

CHAPTER IX

NOTHING IS WRONG WITH THE WORLD
Loving The World

Have You Ever Asked Yourself, *"Why Is The World In Such a Mess?"*

Every generation thinks that the world is getting worse. I love watching movies from the 1950s when this was such a predominant theme – kids were becoming wild because of rock and roll, and the end of the world was at hand because of the atomic bomb.

Every day the newspapers, TV (especially the 24-hour news cycle), and talk radio devote hour after hour and page after page to establishing what a terrible state the world is in. But like everything we've been talking about in this book, it is, or it isn't – depending on how you decide to look at it.

How I Went from Thinking That the World Is a Mess to Thinking That Things Are Getting Better and Better

I grew up in a politically active home. I was eight years old in 1960 when John F. Kennedy ran for President. My parents were staunch Democrats (and Catholics), and they did a lot of work for JFK and other Democratic candidates in Iowa. I helped by stuffing envelopes and licking stamps. I even remember riding in a caravan through Iowa towns while singing, "Hooray for Kennedy!" on a loud speaker as we drove through the streets. We were overjoyed when he was elected.

I'll never forget sitting with my dad the Friday night that President Kennedy was assassinated. For some reason, it was just the two of us watching TV. They showed pictures of JFK with his kids, and we both had tears streaming down our faces.

Because I grew up during the Cold War, I had a very deep fear of a nuclear holocaust and Communism. One of my most vivid recollections is having drills in school for what to do in the event of a nuclear attack. Here was the drill: 1- Get under your desk. 2- Cover your head with your hands. Later in college I saw a poster that added 3- Kiss your ass good-bye!

I was especially afraid of Communism because the nuns told us that if the Communists took over, they would do to Catholics in America what they were doing to Catholics in China. Over there, if you didn't renounce your Catholic faith, they would jab chopsticks under your fingernails and then they would kill you. I had never seen a chopstick before, but I knew that was going to hurt, and I didn't want it to happen to me!

I came of age in the late '60s and early '70s when political revolution was rampant, and I was completely against the Vietnam War. I attended anti-war demonstrations on campus and then worked as a volunteer for George McGovern and our liberal Congressional candidate, Ed Mezvinsky.

I moved to Washington, D.C. when my first husband was in law school and got a job working as a personal assistant for Congressman Mezvinsky who was on the Judiciary Committee during the Watergate impeachment process (Ed's son, Marc, is now married to Chelsea Clinton). It was an exciting time to be in Washington.

Politics was something that my dad and I talked about all of the time until he died. I miss having those discussions with him because they were lively and fun, but now the discussions would be very different.

What about war, poverty, terrorism, pollution, etc., etc. – How can you say that Nothing Is Wrong in those situations?

There are many things in the world that are far from perfect and far from how I desire them to be. But another thing that I truly believe with all of my heart is this:

The World Is Better Off Today Than It Ever Was

It amazes me when people talk about how the world is so much worse now than it "used to be". What I find is that people who say this generally have never studied much history. And, of course, Nothing Is Wrong with that, but it's interesting to see what happens when you gain some perspective.

For example, just a little over 100 years ago, a slave master could starve or kill a slave – another human being – for any reason. I know that slavery still exists today, but it's covert and the general consensus is that no one should be enslaved. This is a major step forward.

A few hundred years ago, millions of people died from starvation and the prevailing thought was it was their own fault and they were not being shown mercy by God. I know that there are still people who die from starvation, but it is no longer just an accepted idea.

During World War II, just 60 years ago, over 50 million people died – and six million of them were Jews, Gypsies, homosexuals, and political dissidents who were rounded up and exterminated just for existing. I know that there are still wars, but not on the same scale as World War II.

There is a level of caring for our fellow human beings that has emerged fairly recently from a historical perspective. Almost all industrialized nations provide health care and basic education for their citizens.

More and more of the world at large recognizes the importance of tolerance and freedom and human rights. We still have work to do, but the arc of history shows that the world really is getting better and better.

The World Can Be Changed by Taking Inspired Action

Back in the 1970s and 1980s when I was so politically active, I was fighting AGAINST everything. And, as we've discussed throughout this book, that never works. After all, what we focus on expands. What we think about gets bigger.

For example:

The US declared a war on drugs, and all that's happened is that there are now more drugs than ever before and huge numbers of people in prison for drug-related offenses.

The US declared a war on poverty, and all we've gotten is more poverty. There are more people living below the poverty line now than there were just ten years ago.

Mother Teresa was once invited to participate in an anti-war rally. She responded, "When you have a peace rally, let me know and I'll be there."

I believe in what Gandhi said, "Be the change you want to see in the world." I truly believe that as people take inspired action, things will continue to improve.

Stepping Stone #9 - Five-Minute Deep Breathing Meditation

Even if you have never meditated, it is an extremely powerful practice that can help you immensely. The combination of silence and deep breathing will bring you into a state of peace and calm about the world and everything else in your life.

As soon as possible after you wake up in the morning, sit in a position that keeps your spine straight. If you need pillows to prop you up, that's fine. If you can do it in your bed, that's easiest and you can do it immediately. If you're going to disturb the person next to you (or fall back asleep), then go somewhere else.

Set a timer for five minutes (your smartphone will work well for this) to avoid thoughts such as, "Has it been five minutes yet? How long has it been?" that intrude on your meditation. You will have those thoughts, to be sure, but knowing that the alarm is set will definitely decrease some of that chatter.

Start breathing deeply. If it helps you to cut the mind chatter, say to yourself, "Breathe in, breathe out," or, "I'm breathing in peace (or whatever you want to breathe in), I'm breathing out frustration (or upset, or worry, or whatever you want to breathe out)." Keep breathing deeply and slowly for the entire five minutes.

I personally prefer to breathe in and out through the nose. Some people prefer breathing in through the nose and out through the mouth. Do whatever feels the best to you and brings you into a deeper space.

This meditation is powerful for a couple of different reasons. Because you are breathing so deeply, you are bringing huge amounts of energy into your body. This is also referred to as "chi" or "prana". This is life energy that fills both your physical body and your etheric body (the energy body that extends approximately 7" from your physical body). It will literally connect you to the energy of All That Is.

Use this time to ask questions and listen for the answers. Use this time to ask what your body or your relationship needs. Use this time to ask, "What is my life purpose?" Use this time to ask, "What is the action that I'm inspired to take in the world?" Or, you can just sit in silence.

This simple five minutes can bring you into the state of Bliss Out faster than anything I know.

Using the Stepping Stones on the Journey to Happy

Stepping Stone #1 – What's Your Story

Are there more thoughts or issues about how you perceive the world that you want to add to your Awareness List? If so, take a deep breath and add them now.

Stepping Stone #2 – Change Your Story, Change Your Life

Stop talking about how terrible the world is and start talking about the awe-inspiring things that are happening each day.

Stepping Stone #3 – The Enneagram Fit

Concerning the general condition of the world, the Enneagram has more to do with how we think things should be "fixed". For all of the Styles, the healing comes from understanding that Nothing Is Wrong.

- **Style One – The Perfectionist**
  Let it be okay that everything isn't perfect and start seeing how things are getting better.

- **Style Two – The Helper**
  Let it be okay that you can't fix everything all by yourself.

- **Style Three – The Achiever**
  You are generally optimistic, so cultivate that type of thinking about the state of the world.

- **Style Four – The Romantic Adventurer**
  Tap into your compassionate nature and understand that everyone is doing the best that they can do with what they have.

- **Style Five – The Investigator**
  Let it be okay that you don't have all of the answers to fix everything.

- **Style Six – The Loyalist**
  Your loyalty can go a long way to support any cause for which you decide to take inspired action.

- **Style Seven – The Enthusiast**
  Your enthusiasm can go a long way to support any cause for which you decide to take inspired action. Just stay focused.

- **Style Eight – The Aggressor**
  Use your righteous anger to fight the good fight, but come from a place of inspired corrective action, not pushing against the object of the fight.

- **Style Nine – The Peacemaker**
  Don't ignore what's going on in the world. Use your peacemaking skills to make the world a better place.

Stepping Stone #4 – Discover the Patterns

What did your parents think about the state of the world? Can you see patterns? Were your parents optimistic or pessimistic? Do you belong to the same political party, or were they not politically interested? Did they think that people are basically good or that people are basically bad? How are you living out those patterns? Which ones would benefit you if you were to leave them behind?

Stepping Stone #5 – *"Loving Your Body"* Meditation

Continue doing the *"Loving Your Body"* Meditation each day. Feeling good in your body makes you feel better about everything, especially how you perceive the world.

Stepping Stone #6 – Gratitude Journal

Each day as you're writing your "High Five", add something to be grateful about concerning the state of the world:

1. I'm grateful that the sun comes up each morning.
2. I'm grateful that the world is so incredibly beautiful.
3. I'm grateful that I live in a place where I can pretty much do or say whatever I want.

Stepping Stone #7 – Tapping Out Your Fears

Use both the short form and the long form. When you're feeling particularly negative, tap through each spot saying, "Even though the world is a terrible place, I deeply and profoundly love, accept, and respect myself just the way I am."

Using the short form (tapping the karate chop point and saying, "I deeply and profoundly love, accept, and respect myself just the way I am.") can have a profound effect on bringing you back into a place of peace and balance.

Stepping Stone #8 – Affirmations

If the state of the world is worrying you, using Affirmations properly can start to rewire your brain around that thinking. Just remember the guidelines:

1. Write the Affirmation as a positive statement.

2. Make it a personal statement. Use "I".

3. Write the Affirmation in the present tense.

4. Stay in a positive space when you are writing the Affirmations:

a) Feel good while you're doing it. If it doesn't feel good, stop doing it.

b) Make it as specific as possible without feeling like you are making it up.

c) Believe that there is at least a kernel of truth in what you're writing.

I'm NOT saying that the world is perfect. I'm not saying that things can't be better. What I AM saying is that if the majority of people acted as a result of inspired action, things could change very quickly. Find something that inspires you and "be the change you want to see in the world".

And now, let's put it all together!

CHAPTER X

30-DAY ACTION PLAN FOR YOUR JOURNEY TO HAPPY

Here is a distillation of everything we've covered. It's your 30-day action plan for your Journey to Happy:

1. Get a new journal. Don't use one with old energy. Get a small, inexpensive one or a beautiful one that makes you feel good every time you see it.

2. Read two chapters each week and complete the processes – you will have finished the book in 30 days.

3. Stop to complete each Stepping Stone, because each process builds on the next:

   1) What's Your Story?
   2) Change Your Story, Change Your Life
   3) Take the Enneagram test – which Style are you?
   4) Discover The Patterns – how did your parents "do" this?
   5) *"Loving Your Body"* Meditation
   6) Gratitude Journal
   7) Tapping
   8) Affirmations
   9) Deep Breathing Meditation

And here's another bonus – if you haven't already, watch my *"Sedona Chakra Meditation"* video to balance your chakras

or go to: http://thejourneytohappy.com/video4/

CHAPTER XI
FINAL THOUGHTS

Remember the 51% Rule

When I first started on my spiritual path, one of the things that I was lucky enough to figure out was what I call the 51% Rule. Simply stated, the 51% Rule acknowledges that, with all this stuff you're trying to do and this energy you're trying to move, if you just stay on the path of your Journey to Happy at least 51% of the time, you're going to have an amazing, incredible life.

You don't have to be perfect. Sometimes you'll be at 60%, other times at 20% – because you're human. But, as you learn to stay in the energy of excited expectation a majority of the time, you'll hit the tipping point and be over the edge. And when that happens, you'll have momentum on your side.

If you haven't already, watch my video *"The 51% Rule"*

or go to: http://thejourneytohappy.com/video5/

A Word of Encouragement

In this book, I've distilled what took me almost forty years to figure out. I hope that you won't take that long. The processes here work. I urge you to start with them today. They take time, but the effort is incredibly rewarding.

Of course, reading a book about clearing energetic blocks and "gunk" is not the same as working one-on-one with a practitioner who has been doing this work for over 20 years.

Many of you will not want to wait for your new life to start. If that describes you, then I urge you to consider doing a Sedona Soul Adventures retreat. What can happen in three or four days is almost unbelievable. Even after 14 years and thousands of people, I'm still amazed by the results.

If it feels right to you, **Use the code** to arrange a free consultation with one of our Angel Guides who will connect with you (or both of you, if a couple) and custom design your retreat for exactly what you need.

or go to:
https://souladventures.infusionsoft.com/app/form/jth

Watch a video with one of our Angel Guides talking about the custom retreat process.

or go to:
http://sedonasouladventures.com/angel-guide-video/

Don't wait to take action! I firmly believe that we are here on this planet to experience love and joy and peace. It's available to each and every one of us, but it's up to us to make it happen.

If not now, then when?

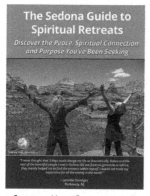

To download a free copy of our *"Sedona Guide to Spiritual Retreats"*

or go to:
http://sedonasouladventures.com/personal-retreat-guide/jth

Watch a video of me talking about why our retreats are so different.

or go to:
http://sedonasouladventures.com/retreat-guides-jth/

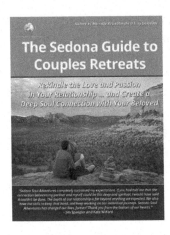

To download a free copy of our *"Sedona Guide to Couples Retreats"*

or go to:
sedonasouladventures.com/couples-retreat-guide/jth/

Watch a video of me talking about our Couples Retreats.

or go to:
http://sedonasouladventures.com/retreats/couples-retreats/

Watch videos of our clients talking about their Soul Adventures (why they came, what happened and the long term effects).

or go to:
http://sedonasouladventures.com/clients-talking-soul-adventures/

CHAPTER XII

WHAT IS A VORTEX
(and Why Should You Care)?

I can't end my book without talking a little bit about the Sedona Vortexes.

Sedona is one of the most beautiful places on the planet (a few years ago, USA Today named Sedona "The most beautiful place to visit in the US".) But beyond its beauty, Sedona is known throughout the world for its vortex energy.

What is a vortex? A vortex is believed to be a special spot on the planet where higher dimensional energies are concentrated to such an extent that it can be felt by humans. These energies enhance the flow of energy (life force) in our own bodies - what the Chinese call "chi", or the Hindus "prana".

Vortexes (or vortices if you want to be absolutely proper about it, but here in Sedona we all pretty much say "vortexes") are found at sacred sites throughout the world – the Great Pyramid in Egypt, Machu Picchu in Peru, Bali, Stonehenge, etc. Many people believe that the vortex energies and the energy that flows through our subtle bodies is basically the same - that it is an electro-magnetic energy.

In my experience, when you delve into definitions and explanations of what a vortex is, it seems to depend on who you're talking to or what book you're reading. If you speak with some scientists, they will tell you that this is electro- magnetic energy that can be measured but that it is behaving in ways that are unusual and can't be explained.

If you speak with the indigenous peoples, e.g., the Native Americans here in Sedona or the Aborigines in Australia (because Ayers Rock (Uluru) is another one), they will tell you that these are places around the Earth where you can literally feel the energy of the Earth if you will take the time to do it.

Here is my own personal belief – after living in Sedona since the turn of the century and having travelled many times to Egypt and Bali and Peru and experiencing those energies – I believe these are places around the world where the God energy (or the energy of the Universe or of All That Is, or whatever you want to call it) literally comes onto the planet and is brought onto the planet. That's why these places are so incredible.

The Native Americans believe that the energy of Sedona is energy that can be used for transformation. And that's why such amazing transformations can happen here in such a short period of time.

The other element of the Sedona energy is that in this special place, everything is amplified, meaning energy is amplified, love is amplified, connection is amplified, disconnection is amplified. Whatever you bring to Sedona is magnified and amplified. Thoughts, feelings, vibrations, whether positive or negative, will be more greatly enhanced and intensified on all the levels – physical, mental, emotional, spiritual.

In addition, the veils to other dimensions are thinner in Sedona. Our connection to All That Is is amplified and enhanced here. Bashar, the internationally recognized spiritual teacher, says this about Sedona:

"Sedona is a powerful, transformational vortex unparalleled in its own way, unique in its own way, that allows for communication and connection to multiple dimensions of reality on your world".

The energies of Sedona are unique – not available anywhere else on the planet.

Why should you care about the Vortex Energy? Because if you're looking for transformation, Sedona is the place to get it. The energy is stronger here, it is the energy of transformation, the veils to other dimensions are thinner (so it's easier to access here) and whatever you bring here is magnified and intensified. This is one of the reasons why people have such huge transformations here in such a short period of time.

The Sedona Effect™

After many years of working with thousands of people here in Sedona I've come to recognize and identify what I now call *The Sedona Effect.*™ The Sedona Effect is a process of transformation that can be accessed by those who have a deep desire to bring this kind of conscious transformation into their lives. The Sedona Effect is the result of three different types of energy coming together in a special way to make transformation and permanent change possible.

The Sedona Effect comes from the combination of three things:

1) the incredible vortex energy of Sedona;
2) the amazing practitioners who have been called to Sedona from all over the planet to do their work and who know how to connect with and utilize this energy, and
3) the intense desire of those coming to Sedona to effect a life-changing transformation.

We've already talked about the first aspect, the incredibly powerful and transformational energy of Sedona. The second aspect of the Sedona Effect, is that healers from all over the world have been drawn here to do their work. Here at Sedona Soul Adventures, our healers have come from England, Germany, South Africa, Ireland, the Netherlands, Australia and of course from all over the United States. In speaking to any of them, you will always hear an incredible story of how they were called to Sedona. My favorite stories are ones about people who were from a completely different background – an airline pilot, an accountant, a medical doctor, a high fashion model, or in my case, an attorney. Suddenly, something happened where the awareness came that life had to be changed and the change was made.

But most important, these are people who know how to connect with this energy and to utilize it for transformation.

The third aspect of the Sedona Effect is the deep desire of people who come here for transformation to happen in their lives. It is a palpable, powerful force of energy.

Even if you are in turmoil, or especially if you are in turmoil, this is an energy that is huge and real. It is deep and when it is happening, the person can sometimes feel like they're ready to jump out of their skin.

That's what happened to me the first time I came to Sedona. I felt like I was literally ready to jump out of my skin. I knew I had to do something; I just didn't know what that something was. I also didn't know that this uncomfortable, (almost) painful feeling was actually something powerful that was pushing me and moving me. As I look back now, this was truly the Highest part of my Self shoving me toward the transformations that were in store.

So I came to Sedona for what I thought would be 3 days of just being quiet. Instead, what happened was The Sedona Effect. I brought the energy of my deep desire, I did healing work with an incredible practitioner and the energy of the Mother literally came to me with the message that I must change my life. That if I didn't, I was going to die. I listened to the message. My life was completely transformed because of The Sedona Effect.

Thank you for letting me share my story with you.

Many blessings,
Debra Stangl
Sedona, Arizona

If you haven't already, watch my video *"The Sedona Effect"*

or go to: http://thejourneytohappy.com/video6/

ABOUT DEBRA STANGL

Debra Stangl is an example of how life is full of second chances. In 1999, she was a divorce attorney in Omaha, Nebraska, hating her work, depressed, 40 pounds overweight, and in an unhappy marriage. Through a strange set of circumstances, she came to the spiritual mecca of Sedona, Arizona for the first time and experienced a spiritual reawakening that changed her life.

She closed her law practice, and over the next three years, traveled back to Sedona over and over again, pursuing her own personal healing work with the amazing practitioners who have been drawn to Sedona from all over the world.

In 2001, just two weeks before 9/11, Debra received the message that she was supposed to move to Sedona. She followed the instructions, and six months later started Sedona Soul Adventures. Drawing from her own personal experience of coming to Sedona to heal, Debra realized that the healing came from utilizing the unique energy of Sedona and working one-on-one with different practitioners on different aspects of her healing process. Through the vehicle of Sedona Soul Adventures, she developed the unique process of deeply transformational, customized retreats for individuals and couples. Since then, the lives (and relationships) of thousands of people have been transformed through the work of Sedona Soul Adventures.

In the past 14 years, Debra has also developed a unique process called Transformational Life Coaching which combines traditional forms of personal coaching with intuition and vibrational alignment. The result is that clients have experienced huge transformations in every area of their life – including their work and careers, physical health and well-being, personal relationships, money, etc.

Debra also leads group trips each year to Egypt and Peru, allowing participants to connect with the energies of these sacred places. If you would like information about these sacred journeys,

Use the code

or go to:
http://sedonasouladventures.com/sacred-travel-video-jth/

Debra received her Bachelor's Degree in Theatre and Dance from the University of Iowa in 1974. After that, she lived in Washington, D.C. and was the personal assistant to Congressman Edward Mezvinsky, who was on the Judiciary Committee during the Watergate proceedings (and is now Chelsea Clinton's father-in-law).

Next, she was the personal assistant to former Supreme Court Justice Abe Fortas who encouraged her to go to law school. Debra graduated from Creighton Law School in 1979 and practiced law in Omaha, Nebraska.

During that time, she was an advocate for women and children and wrote the "Children's Trust Fund Act" which is legislation that funds programs for the prevention of child abuse. For her efforts, she was named one of ten "Outstanding Young Omahans" in 1982 and the "Outstanding Young Nebraskan" by the statewide Nebraska Chamber of Commerce in 1983. Debra practiced law for 20 years before her spiritual reawakening led her to leave her practice and come to Sedona.

Since founding Sedona Soul Adventures in 2002 and helping thousands of people transform their lives and relationships, Debra writes and speaks about how it is possible to live a life of joy and ease and purpose.

www.SedonaSoulAdventures.com

Sedona Soul Adventures

Watch More Videos

What is a vortex?

or go to: http://sedonasouladventures.com/vortex/

Watch videos of some of our practitioners talking about their work

or go to: http://sedonasouladventures.com/watch-videos-practitioners-talking-work/

Watch Debra talking about why Sedona Soul Adventures is different

or go to: http://sedonasouladventures.com/retreat-guides-jth/

**Watch Debra talking about coming to
Sedona for the first time**

or go to: http://sedonasouladventures.com/debras-
transformation-jth/

**Watch Debra talking about how to have the perfect
Sedona Soul Adventure (just "show up")**

or go to: http://sedonasouladventures.com/debra/

**Watch videos of our clients talking about their Sedona
Soul Adventures retreat – (why they came, what
happened and the long term effects)**

or go to: http://sedonasouladventures.com/clients-
talking-soul-adventures/

Watch video on Sacred Travel

or go to: http://sedonasouladventures.com/sacred-travel-video-jth/

Egypt trip video

or go to: http://sedonasouladventures.com/sacred-travel/egypt-tours/retreat-guides-jth/

Machu Picchu & Peru trip

or go to: http://sedonasouladventures.com/sacred-travel/peru-tours/jth/